Letters from Art

ART HAWKINS

Standing Tall in the Shadow of

ALDO LEOPOLD

Letters from Art

ART HAWKINS
Standing Tall in the Shadow of
ALDO LEOPOLD

by
Art Hawkins
as told to
Ken M. Blomberg

Ten | 16
PRESS
www.ten16press.com - Waukesha, WI

Letters From Art: Art Hawkins Standing Tall in the Shadow of Aldo Leopold
Copyrighted © 2019, 2020 Ken M. Blomberg
ISBN 978-1-64538-008-5
Library of Congress Control Number: 2019935752
Letters From Art: Art Hawkins Standing Tall in the Shadow of Aldo Leopold
by Ken M. Blomberg
Second Edition

For information, please contact:

Ten | 16
PRESS

www.ten16press.com
Waukesha, WI

Cover design by Therese Joanis

This book was written in memory of
Art and Betty Hawkins
and dedicated to their children
Amy, Tex and Ellen

FOREWORD

Aldo Leopold wrote that "there are two things that interest me, the relationship of people to land and people to each other". This seemingly simple statement is in ways a "catch all" to the point of being almost trite, if not for being exemplified so well by Leopold's life. He knew better than anyone the extent of our collective ignorance about the inner workings of land and made remarkable contributions in turning that around, which alone would have constituted an extraordinary life and work. However, Leopold also knew that care for land inherently required care for one another. In an extension of this thinking, Leopold wrote in an unpublished essay that included, "The basic question in conservation is not the condition of the land, but the proportion of people who love it". In short, Leopold understood the important human complexities involved in any worthwhile enterprise, particularly in the slow, laborious process of reorienting human attitudes toward land. The importance of the human complexities was not limited to the general public in matters of land, but arguably amplified by orders of magnitude with Leopold's own colleagues, students and family.

By fortuitous chance, I have a somewhat unique relationship to both the author and subject of this book. I initially met Ken while looking for my first bird dog – a German Shorthair Pointer. I was starting my graduate work on woodcock and thought I ought to have a bird dog to help my days afield. Ken had a litter, with pups still available - and in that first encounter I expanded my family and world in ways I could not have imagined. As it happened, Ken's son Erik came to work with my research field crew for the next three years between his semesters at the local University. So, began another lifelong friendship. And Ken's numerous published writings have brought me great joy over the years.

I cannot recall the first time I met Art Hawkins. He was in ways always an extension of our family – if not in person, in shared stories and history. I do remember well the warmth of his character and brightness he carried with him and shared in every encounter, no matter how brief or extended. He was a beautiful human being and it was immediately evident.

As an ecologist and Leopold's great grandson, I also share with Art a unique place in an extraordinary legacy. Following in the footsteps of a giant such as Leopold is a hefty affair to say the least. I certainly felt the weight, especially as a young person without a clear direction. Rolling up your sleeves and working hard is certainly part of the equation to finding one's way, but in my case, I was lucky to find a mentor who genuinely cared for me and helped build me up personally and professionally. I am certain that without this care my achievements *and* connection to place would be more limited.

In my work we attribute shade tolerance to trees. We often gloss over the fact that completely shade intolerant trees often do better as seedlings under the shade of parent trees – only to eventually assume, and require, full sunlight. It is easy to imagine that Art felt the shadow of working directly under a giant like Leopold. What these letters and stories do is to give us a glimpse of the nurturing and care involved in that process. They also give us an unfiltered behind the scenes look at the always interesting course of growing into greatness, which there is no question Art Hawkins did.

Ken has expertly provided to us a unique view of history, and examples of relationships forged between people and land and to each other through the personal letters and stories of Art Hawkins. Through ordinary accounts of an extraordinary life, we are treated to a rich narrative of humanity and beauty. Not just to the evolution of Art Hawkins, including Leopold's role in this, but to the evolution of Leopold's thinking through his students, especially Art Hawkins. A clear example of this was Art's quail research at Faville Grove. Art set out to investigate expanding quail populations and ranges only to see them sharply curtailed in subsequent severe winters – despite artificially provided food and cover. Leopold, who once spoke of "a new and objective equilibrium" in place of a natural one, now recognized that wildlife management had "admitted its inability to replace natural equilibria with artificial ones, and its unwillingness to do so even if it could". Leopold's faith in management had been shaken and this set forth a very different path for both Leopold and Hawkins. Stemming from this experience Leopold began to recognize Faville Grove as "an excellent place to make a really serious test of the idea of reconnecting people with land." Art had no small part in this endeavor. He, along with so many others changed history and gave us firm footing from which to do well by land and each other. Art certainly stood tall, and we are all better for it.

Jed Meunier
22 February 2019

INTRODUCTION

My introduction to Art happened quite by accident.

While attending a Leopold Education Project (LEP) annual conference sponsored by Pheasants Forever (PF) in Baraboo, Wisconsin during the summer of 2002 I met his daughter, Amy. On the first day of the three-day weekend event, we met during an LEP Educator Workshop. During a round-table introduction period I mentioned I was a writer and raised German Shorthaired Pointers (GSPs). Later that day we ended up partners in a breakout session and engaged in small talk.

She shared that her father was Art Hawkins, one of the first graduate students under Aldo Leopold - and in fact had given Aldo Leopold a shorthair puppy named "Gus". I mentioned my attempt to trace Gus's lineage to see if descendants of this now famous dog still existed. She ended by saying her father loved GSPs and would enjoy talking to me about Gus. I gave her my business card with a note and asked if she'd pass it along.

A few weeks later, on September 2, 2002, I received Art's first letter from Hugo, Minnesota.

It began,

"Dear Ken: This is in response to the note on the card you gave Amy Donlin to give me about the German Pointer "Gus". His name on the pedigree was Gotz von Tubengen if I spelled it right..."

The entire letter appears in Chapter 2.

I put on my detective clothes and with the help of one of the most knowledgeable GSP historians, Bob Check, of Stevens Point, Wisconsin produced a multi-generation pedigree. That information and later, a visit to Hugo to interview Art, led to an article I wrote later that year called, "In Search of Gus". It was subsequently published in a national magazine The Pointing Dog Journal out of Traverse City, Michigan. That article also appears as Chapter 2 in this book.

Art's last letter came on March 10, 2006, the day after an email from Amy. Her note began, "I'm writing to you all in a state of shock. I don't know how to break news like this since thankfully I've never done it before – we're all pretty numb. So, I guess I'll just tell you that today at around 4 pm we lost dad."

You see, her father, Art Hawkins, had passed away on March 9, 2006 at the age of 92. His last letter found my mailbox on March 10th, the day after his passing. It was dated March 7th. Classic Art – it was a two-pager, handwritten on legal paper – beginning and ending with warm pleasantries.

"Dear Ken, The busy weekend is over. Ours went well. How about yours? The Pembletons were here the night before they left for Wisconsin. They planned to visit 4 of the "Read Leopolds" and regretted not being able to fit in yours. I shared your letter with them...Our landscape is white from a recent half-incher, but bare spots will appear later today if the temp reaches 35 degrees or so...Woodcock are due back any day now...a few geese are back but no robins or blackbirds yet...Best wishes, Art."

Amy discovered her father two days later near their barn with walking sticks still in hand and binoculars around his neck. He had spent much of the spring day hiking and observing wildlife on their nature preserve property. From a bench overlooking their marsh, he, granddaughter Piper and companion dog Koko watched spring geese and ducks milling around on the lake.

Amy e-mailed, "We're all in disbelief, but a comfort is that dad left so much the way his mentor, Aldo Leopold did – suddenly, and without lingering illness or suffering and after having such a great hike, on a blue-sky day, his ducks and geese all around returning for another nesting season, we're sure that's the way he hoped it would go…and what he'd want, is for all of us to read Leopold's A Sand County Almanac (again) and do the right thing for the land and the wetlands and the air we breathe."

Today, I sit at my desk, surrounded by letters from Art (I kept them all) and contemplate my assignment – a book paying tribute to a great man, who stood tall in the shadow of greatness. You'll see. Read on.

Much of this book was written by Art. His letters, letters to Art from Aldo, transcripts from lectures as well as columns and essays he wrote over the years. To the end, he championed the Leopold Land Ethic.

I just returned from turning the dogs out of the kennel office. I was greeted by a pair of geese flying overhead, honking and proclaiming spring is finally here – after an extremely long, persistent winter. Perhaps a message from Art?

This book is my humble attempt to reply to Art's last letter, now more than a decade later.

Ken M. Blomberg
Junction City, Wisconsin
15 March 2018

ACKNOWLEDGMENTS

First and foremost, I'd like to recognize and thank Art Hawkins for his writing talent, his meticulous habit of saving documents, attention to details, warm and welcoming attention to this scribbler and an unwavering memory - right up to the end of his extraordinary life. And to his wife Betty, for sharing insightful details of their life together - from Wisconsin's Faville Grove, to Illinois, to Texas, to Manitoba and eventually to Hugo, Minnesota. I would like to thank Ed and Sil Pembleton, who led me to Art through their dedication to the Leopold Education Project (LEP), Ed's magic hand at photography, and Sil's love of all things wild and free. To Amy Hawkins Donlin. Our chance meeting at that first LEP workshop led me on the path from Baraboo to Hugo, where I was able to gather the majority of the information found in this book. Thanks to you and your parents hospitality as I dug through Art's files. And to Arthur "Tex" Hawkins and Ellen Hawkins Brandenburg, who also allowed me to peek into their family history.

To the U.S. Fish and Wildlife Service for sharing Art's contribution in the book *Flyways - Pioneering Waterfowl Management in North America* and Mark Madison of the USFWS History for allowing me to use excerpts from his oral history interviews with Art and Betty.

And to Jed Meunier, great-grandson of Aldo Leopold, who wrote the Foreword to this book.

CONTENTS

1

LETTERS FROM ART

A rt Hawkins and I exchanged somewhere in the neighborhood of 40 letters between September 2, 2002 and March 7, 2006. Art, from the "Greatest Generation", was a scholar, a veteran, a waterfowl biologist, a conservationist and an accomplished writer. Under the wings of his poetic professor and sometimes editor Aldo Leopold, he learned to turn a phrase, teach and communicate in a way that unfortunately, in this day and age, has disappeared. I was so touched, so moved by his old school handwritten letters and heartfelt words that I saved them all – not knowing at the time they were destined for this book. To those who care about such things, I share his letters and much more.

Several letters to and from his professor, colleagues and friends, as well as excerpts from books, transcripts from lectures, columns and essays make up much of what follows in these pages. His first letters to me (captured in Chapter 2) dealt mostly with Leopold's famous German Shorthaired Pointer named Gus. The others are scattered throughout the book to illustrate this man's most fascinating life – like the following:

September 24, 2002

Hi Ken:
Thought you might like this clipping. In your work on woodcock did you ever get mauled by a bear? I never associated bears and woodcock but can see how it would happen.
I understand that there are no native earthworms in the glaciated area. Wonder what timberdoodles ate before exotic worms took over?
Art

In this short, two-paragraph note he asked two questions. "Asking questions," Art told me, "was a teaching method Professor Leopold used on his students." And Art's questions worked on me. If a woodcock's diet is predominately (90%) earthworms, what in fact did they eat before European worms repopulate the northern stretches of their range? Several textbooks on earthworms have since joined my personal library. Below is an excerpt from my September 30, 2002 reply to his questions. I also enclosed a copy of a monthly magazine column I wrote at the time, *Kennel Talk*, that mentioned woodcock.

Dear Art,
No, I never encountered a bear while banding woodcock! But, my dogs and I have been distressed by a couple over the years while hunting woodcock. Opening weekend this year, a wolf followed us out of the woods. That was quite exciting...
Ken

The next month Art continued the woodcock discussion in the following letter:

October 3, 2002

Dear Ken:
Your article in Kennel Talk *telling of your first experience with woodcock reminded me of mine – not 30 years ago, but more like 75. At the time I lived in Batavia, N.Y. (between Buffalo and Rochester). I had a paper route and one evening a customer who knew I was interested in birds told me about some strange looking birds they'd seen in the woods back of their place. They had long bills and had a whistle when they flew. I knew they had to be woodcock. After completing my route, I got my gun, a single barrel 30" La Fever single full choke and some #4 shells (the only ones I had on hand) and with my young Eng. Pointer Richmond Pep walked to the nearby woods. I followed a recently brushed-out powerline through the thicket of aspen and some thorn apples. Soon I flushed a woodcock and, as I recall, shot 3 before it got too dark. These were the first game birds I ever shot, since this was my first hunting season.*
My dad was not a hunter and it was my grandfather who got me my first gun and my mother who allowed me to get my bird dog...
Best wishes,
Art Hawkins

On May 29, 2003, after my article on Leopold's Gus (see Chapter 2) was finished, Art wrote and thanked me for *"my great detective work plus interesting article."* But in his flair of good old storytelling he added a few paragraphs of his family's own goings on...

Hi Ken:

Betty and I spent the past week end with our daughter Ellen in the Superior National Forest where she, Rick and young Willie live. We weren't the only visitor. About sunset one evening, Betty headed for the outhouse when across her path ran a furry animal. When she told Ellen, Willie and me, who were inside, we all ran out in hopes of seeing it. Betty went out on the deck which overlooks a grassy patch (lawn) with the woods behind. She was surprised when out of the woods came the animal.

The lynx sat down on the grassy patch and looked at Betty from 20' away. Then it leisurely departed around the west side of the house but still in view of Betty until hidden by some bushes.

Ellen puts out bird feed which attracts snowshoes, squirrels and chipmunks as well as birds. Two nights earlier we heard a fox barking nearby which Ellen thought might be at a bear but now we think it was the lynx.

While there we also saw a spruce grouse and a ruffed grouse drumming at close range among the 50 birds we recorded including woodcock and snipe. It was a good weekend and bugless.

Best wishes,
Art and the Lynx lady, Betty

We exchanged three more letters that year, another one in the summer, one that fall and one just before Christmas on December 23rd. What follows here is his holiday greeting and "lynx update" letter. Note the report on his never-ending quest to make a difference on the environmental front. Even at 89 years old he was an inspiration, attending meetings and working on issue papers with fellow conservationists.

Dear Ken:

I enjoyed your account of hunting experiences this fall which shows how place and timing mean everything when it comes to hunting. Another friend who hunts regularly in N.D. commented on how unusually bad it was for him this fall.

I've been busy with ducks all fall in a different capacity than with a scatter gun. The enclosed article from <u>Outdoor News</u> tells about this activity. If you take Outdoor News (Wisconsin Edition) maybe you saw it. At any rate we met again yesterday to work on a position paper which when finished will be sent to the proper authorities. Any comments you may have based on the news story would be appreciated.

Our "kids" from up north have arrived for the holidays full of stories about the critters that inhabit the woods around their house which is surrounded by the Superior Nat. Forest. (Ellen and Rich both work for the Forest Service in the BWCAW.) The most exciting stories recently have been about lynx. They had one sunning itself in their bird feeding area beside their house about Thanksgiving time. Earlier this fall another lynx was feeding on a deer it had killed. They reported it to a DNR team studying the rare cat. They came out, trapped the 28# male and now it wears a radio.

We hope you all are having a Merry Christmas and drop by when you can.

Art Hawkins

In 2004 we exchanged letters only two times. The Hawkins family farm was loaded with wood duck nest boxes, many clustered in their backyard on the shores of the lake their land bordered. That and Art's dedication and leadership with the Wood Duck Society based out of Twin Cities, Minnesota inspired me to apply and receive a grant through my employer at the time, the Wisconsin Rural Water Association (WRWA) and co-sponsoring Wisconsin Waterfowl Association (WWA). Called the Rural Water Wood Duck Research (RWWDR) project, it involved placing wood duck boxes across Wisconsin near community wastewater lagoons. I wrote Art with the news and that prompted the following speedy reply:

Dear Ken:

Congratulations on getting the Besadny grant for the RWWDR project. (How do you pronounce that?) I note that the letter and check is signed by Charlie Luthin. Did you know that he used to have Buddy Huffaker's job as Ex. Sec. for the AL Foundation? The Wood Duck Society will be interested in this project and its findings. Do you belong to the W.D. Society? If not and you want to join send me $10 and I'll sign you up. You may want to contribute a short article about your project for the Wood Duck Newsgram (3 issues per year).

Yes, I told Ed Pembleton that I would participate again, probably on the same basis as last year—only on the final day after a stop-over at Betty's family home near Lake Mills (Faville Grove).

Maybe you could check with Ed about your Gus article and visit here at the same time. Erik's summer job sounds unique and interesting and so does your new acquisition Duke. Maybe Karl can fly you over. There's a landing strip on the east side of Bald Eagle Lake just north of White Bear Lake about 2 miles east of us as the crow flies, but maybe that's rushing things a bit.

We intend to visit Faville Grove this week end if my doc lets me. I've had a bad cough with laryngitis which he says is borderline pneumonia. Someone wants to interview me about

old times. Not good if I can't talk.
Hope to see you if you get over this way.
Best regards,
Art
P.S. Migrating songbirds reached a peak last week end. Tex
was here for his son's graduation from U. of M. and recorded 19
warblers on our place.

Art's reference to our mutual friend Ed involved an upcoming Pheasant Forever sponsored Leopold Education Project (LEP) annual meeting in Baraboo, Wisconsin. For many years in a row Art was a keynote speaker. In 2003 his presentation was about Leopold's classic book Game Management and its influence of his own career in waterfowl management. Also at the time of this letter, I was waiting for word on my article "In Search of Gus" (Chapter 2) which had been submitted to Pheasants Forever. It was rejected, but later accepted and published in nationally distributed Pointing Dog Journal. Art also mentioned my boys Erik and Karl. Erik was an undergraduate student at UW -Stevens Point at the time and was working that summer with Aldo Leopold's great grandson, Jed Meunier on a woodcock radio telemetry project in north central Wisconsin. My younger son, Karl, at age 15 had just received his student pilot license – thus Art's "maybe that's rushing things a bit" comment on him flying me to Bald Eagle Lake airport.

On December 20, 2004 Art wrote the following "catch-up" and season greetings letter:

Dear Ken:
We seem to have lost contact during the past year and perhaps
this is a good time to catch up. I took in the LEP workshop at the

Dells again this year and as usual it was quite an inspiration. For the fourth year I monitored the Pelton Lake heron rookery for the DNR and again it failed. This time we had cameras set up to keep track of several nests when we weren't there. They revealed that coons were taking young off the nests and this activity may have been on a scale causing the birds to desert their colony. I keep active with the Concerned Duck Hunters Panel (CDHP) which got out a report calling for more conservative hunting regulations. So far no actions on our suggestions. I also worked with a group Sportsmen for Kerry. Bush made many visits to Minnesota during the campaign assuring sportsmen that he was their friend and would out-do his dad's no net loss policy regarding wetlands. We shall see.

Now, how about you? Did you and your son band woodcock this year and how is that classy pointer you had at the workshop doing? Our dog Koko is having problems with arthritis. Our Vet has prescribed Deramarex 100 mg 1 tablet every other day and ½ tablet in between. Koko thinks they're great (a treat) but they cost us $3.50 a tablet, that's more than I pay for my own tablets. Do you know of anything cheaper that does the job?

Betty and I have the usual growing old ailments but can't complain. Amy keeps busy at the Wargo Nature Center and Piper does well at school. We wish you all a Merry Christmas and best wishes for '05.

Art Hawkins

I wrote Art back on January 3, 2005:

Dear Art,
Imagine my surprise and delight in receiving a holiday letter from Hugo, Minnesota! Thank you so much for thinking of me

and bringing me up-to-date on you and your family.

More than one person has told me that I missed a great LEP Annual Meeting last summer in the Dells. LEP's Treva Breuch even said "Gus" was talked about and I should have been there. Ed Pembleton said you did a great job once again at this wonderful weekend event. Sorry I missed it.

Speaking of Ed and Gus, I got some disappointing news. Ed informed me that the editor of the Pheasants Forever magazine decided not to publish my article "In Search of Gus". So..., I've decided to send it off to another national magazine for their consideration. It's a great story that needs to be shared, so I'll persist until it's published. In any event, it will always hold a chapter in a book that I'm working on for the future. Another chapter involves the "Grand Tour", a hunting spot in Juneau County that Leopold frequented while grouse and woodcock hunting. I found a map of his from the archives of the University of Wisconsin (see enclosed copy). I was able to physically locate it on one of my road trips and hope to hunt it myself someday. I've included some other pictures of Gus, Aldo and Estella and Gus (at Faville Grove). The one with Gus and the tame crow says the dog (Flick) that replaced Gus was purchased in Feb 1944 from Buido Rahn of Manitowoc, WI. Thought you'd enjoy seeing this.

Our wood duck project got off to a good start with 50 nesting boxes erected in 2004 and another planned to be put up this coming spring. We're working with the Wisconsin Waterfowl Association (WWA) and hope to make this a long-term project.

My oldest son, Erik is in his last semester as a wildlife management major at UW- Stevens Point and will graduate with honors in June. You asked about woodcock banding, well, Erik participated in the third year of a MN, WI and MI woodcock research project with Jed Meunier (Nina Leopold-Bradley's grandson). They banded nearly 150 birds and put radio-telemetry on 125 of those. I got the opportunity to go along on occasion.

Karl, my 16-year-old earned his student's pilot license this past summer and will take his final exam in May. I'll have my own personal pilot to get me places quick! I told him wildlife managers need pilots to do duck surveys and that he should think about a career as a pilot with a state agency.

Sorry to hear about your dog's arthritis. You might like to try a heat pad and aspirin. My Merck Veterinary Manual prescribes 5 to 18 mg/lb body weight daily, or every 8 to 12 hours. They call aspirin the drug of choice for relief of arthritic pain. And I call aspirin much cheaper than the $2.50 per tablet you're buying now. I'm no vet, but it might be worth a try.

Oh, I'm getting more involved with LEP by organizing a Leopold Weekend (March 5-6) event here in Stevens Point. Last year the Gov. and Legislature declared the first weekend in March officially "Aldo Leopold Weekend". Also, I'm working with our state coordinator Treva Bruech on a facilitator/educator workshop near here in April.

Well, that's enough for now. Again, so nice to hear from you – thank you so much for the season's greeting. I'm wondering if I could visit you and Betty around the time the ice goes off your lake? It would be nice to visit, watch the returning ducks and perhaps you could tell me more about your career after Faville Grove. If that works for you, we'll talk as spring approaches.

Ken

On February 3, 2005 Art wrote back. At 91 years old, you can see his mind was still sharp as a tack. Always observant of nature's current goings-on, brimming with memories of the past and still very active in conservation issues of the day. He always filled his letters with leading questions for me – a habit he said that rubbed off from his professor.

Dear Ken:

It's almost time for the first migrant geese to return to southern Wisconsin. Can spring be far behind? I hope you made progress on the book you are writing including the Grand Tour. Do you know of Babcock WI? On a farm near there I had a quail census area in 1935. Yes, quail. I stayed at the CCC camp while working in that area. I also spent several days with Franklin Schimedt trapping prairie chickens on the Cardo Farm near Plainfield.

Will you be attending the waterfowl meeting in Stevens Point the weekend of March 5? One of the speakers (maybe the main one) will be Norman Seymour from Nova Scotia. He will arrive in the Twin Cities on March 3, have dinner at our place and be driven to Stevens Point next day by Dave Zentner. I think that Dave also is on the program. Both of them and I belong to a small group called CDHP concerned duck hunters panel which has prepared a critical statement about duck hunting regulations. My insert will give you some idea of our mission.

I think you would enjoy meeting both of them and if you have a chance to talk, you should tell them your Gus story. Both may have ideas on where to get it published. You could also tell them you and I are connected to the LEP project and you and your son's connection to woodcock. (Both are avid hunters and Norman's experiences include the U.K., Australia & New Zealand. Dave used to be Nat. President of IWLA and Norm is author of the excellent book: Living a Dream, an excellent book on duck hunting and waterfowl management. Norm did grad work at Delta and has written many scientific reports on black ducks.

If you go, I'd like to hear your impressions of the meeting and I hope we can get together this spring.

Best regards;

Art Hawkins

I regret missing the waterfowl conference, but it overlapped a local Aldo Leopold Foundation (ALF) sponsored Leopold Weekend event I was organizing in his honor. I did however, manage a visit to Hugo that spring - and brought Rocky and another of our German shorthairs along for the ride. Art, his wife Betty and daughter Amy were the most gracious of hosts. Good friends Ed and Sil Pembleton joined us for dinner and wine. If memory serves I had my first sip of Japanese sake that day.

Art and I conversed for hours that memorable day at their dining table - strategically positioned by a large picture window overlooking the backyard and beyond, across the expanse of Amelia Lake. As we kept watch over the backyard we observed wood ducks investigating a half dozen nesting boxes, loons swimming by on the lake, pileated woodpeckers feeding at rather large suet feeders, bog islands floating by and a medley of feeding songbirds. We spent a good portion of the day discussing a wide range of subjects – including the professor, Gus, Faville Grove, Manitoba, Hugo, wood ducks, market hunting, and so on and so forth.

Then before I departed, Art suggested I take my dogs for a pheasant survey behind Amy's nearby home - where several acres of prairie grasslands stretched on to the cattail lined shore of the lake. The dogs had a great run, but alas found no pheasants.

No matter, my day was complete notwithstanding. A memorable day I will take to my grave.

In Search of Gus was finally published in 2005. It appeared in the Pointing Dog Journal which is published out of Traverse City, Michigan and distributed nationally. I sent a copy of the finished product to Art in late June and here's his reply on July 3rd:

Dear Ken:

Your article about Gus arrived and it's a dilly! I'm anxious to hear about any reader's responses. I'll bet that the magazine and readers never before saw anything quite like it. Several people I've shown it to have asked for a copy.

You mentioned the possibility of being in the Twin Cities sometime this month. Next week we'll all be gone. Will join our daughter Ellen at Tofte and from there drive along L. Superior to Rossport, Ont. near Nipigon for a few days.

Can it be that the annual LEP workshop is only about 6 weeks away? I've been asked to be there but at 92 one can't be sure. I'm preparing a paper about Leopold's interest and involvement with birds. His favorites were woodcock and grouse. It's fun looking at his writings strictly tied to birds.

We had a surprise this spring when 2 hen turkeys showed up but a much bigger one (surprise) when one of the hens appeared with a brood of 9. When and where she found a gobbler is a mystery.

Recently our lake has treated us to a spectacle of big white birds. A couple of days ago I counted 7 trumpeter swans and 13 pelicans to go with 4 or 5 egrets and a flock of gulls. A flotilla of about 56 Canadas swam by us as they cruised around the lake in their flightless stage and last evening a group of 5 loons swam by and did some hollering. We had our first turkey brood Wow!

July has been pleasantly cool until now. I'm glad we're headed for L. Superior next week.

Thanks for the Gus article and best wishes.

Art Hawkins

That September, Art wrote a short note following the August LEP meeting in Baraboo. I had the honor of sitting in the front row with Art, and if memory serves, helped him shuffle his notes and walking stick as he got up and down during his well-received talk. In addition, I brought our German Shorthaired Pointer male, Rocky, to the meeting at Art's request. You'll understand the reason more clearly after finishing the next chapter.

Hi Ken:

A mite slow in getting this to you, eh? But Amy takes the blame. She just made me a copy.

I sure enjoyed the brief meeting and thanks for taking good care of me.

All goes well here except we aren't seeing many ducks yet. We'll see what happens when the season opens this Sat. Recent rains didn't help the small wetlands but should have improved the sit. for woodcock.

Thanks for showing us your great G. pointer at the meeting. Drop in when you come this way.

Best wishes,

Art

The author and his dog Rocky visit Art at an LEP meeting in Baraboo, Wisconsin.

Fall and winter passed before I heard back from Art in the spring of 2006. He was a master at letter writing. His were always extraordinary – handwritten, two-pagers, full of news on the conservation front, nature's ways and matters related to family – his and mine. His last letter was my favorite. You'll find it later in the book, but before peeking, please read on – and as you'll see, Art Hawkins's life was much, much more than letter writing.

2

IN SEARCH OF GUS

On September 2, 2002 I received my first letter from Art. As I mentioned earlier, I met his daughter Amy at a Leopold Education Project (LEP) workshop in Baraboo, Wisconsin that summer, and discovered Art's relationship to Aldo Leopold and his German Shorthaired Pointer named "Gus". Subsequent to the letter I met with Art several times in Wisconsin and Minnesota and corresponded with him on a regular basis until his passing in 2006.

Dear Ken:

This is in response to the note on the card you gave Amy Dolin to give me about the German pointer "Gus". His name on the pedigree was Gotz von Tubengen if I've spelled it right. I bought Gus in 1936 or possibly 1935 from Joeseph Burkhardt, a dog trainer in St. Croix Falls, Wisconsin. I don't recall how I heard about him but was told that Gus was trained on sharptails. He cost me $50, nearly a month's pay for me at that time. At first Gus was baffled by the running of pheasants but soon caught on. I used him for census work as well as hunting. To my knowledge he never sired pups.

*I gave Gus to Aldo Leopold in 1938 when I moved to a job
with the Ill. Nat. History Survey with no way to keep a dog.
Late in 1943 when I was in the military at Amarillo, Texas Aldo sent
me a copy of his essay Gus's Last Hunt.
Gus must have measured up to Aldo's standards because on
1/20/44 he wrote to Burkhardt as follows: "Gus turned out to be
one of the most brilliant field dogs I ever owned, but I lost him
last November. I am anxious to get a pup of the same strain. If
you are still raising shorthairs, I would like to know what you
have on hand or in prospect. If not, can you forward this letter
to someone whose stock you can recommend as equal to Gus's?"
I lost track after that but perhaps one of Aldo's children could
tell you.*

> *Best wishes,*
> *Art Hawkins*

The following is an article I subsequently wrote about my
search for Leopold's hunting dog named Gus. *In Search of Gus*
was first published in 1991 in the nationally distributed Pointing
Dog Journal magazine. This bird dog played a significant role
in Art's bird census work at Faville Grove and later, became the
Leopold family's companion and hunting dog. I learned Art not
only had Gus's registration papers after all those years, it also
turned out he had a story to tell about a dog the Leopold family
adored. This now famous dog will forever be remembered as
an often mentioned character in Leopold's classic book, *A Sand
County Almanac*. As I mention in the article, as far as I can tell,
no single person, place, or subject is mentioned more often in
the Almanac than Gus.

IN SEARCH OF GUS

This is a story about a bird dog. Not just any bird dog, but arguably one of the world's most famous bird dogs.

I met him more than 30 years ago on the pages of a celebrated book, A Sand County Almanac, written by the legendary biologist and author Aldo Leopold, who had a flair for leaving his readers with more questions than answers. I fell into his trap, yearning to know more about this legendary dog, and the rest of the story.

It began on opening day of the 1936 Wisconsin pheasant hunting season, when a hunting party that consisted of Art Hawkins, of the Faville Grove Wildlife Experimental Area, and University of Wisconsin Professors John Emlen and Aldo Leopold gathered in a farmyard in the south-central part of the state. Leading the way was a bird dog named Gus. Like countless other pheasant hunters across the landscape that day, the group anxiously looked at their watches.

"I released Gus precisely at noon," recalled Art. "He quickly ranged toward a brushy fencerow and disappeared as though on the track of a pheasant."

Art had good reason to impress one of the professors, who had entrusted to him the job of managing the Faville Grove Wildlife Area near Lake Mills. The major task at hand was to census the game bird populations, which consisted of ring-necked pheasants, prairie chickens, Hungarian partridge, bobwhite quail, and, during periods of migration, woodcock and snipe.

"A local sportsman, Sam Kiskow, helped me get started," recollects Art. "Sam was an all-around good sportsman who raised pheasants and Canada geese in the summer and brought about the first pheasant releases in that area. He was a strong believer in winter feeding and maintained several feeding stations."

Kiskow had a bird dog, and he introduced Art to the German shorthaired pointer and Joseph Burkhart, who owned a kennel near St. Croix Falls on the Wisconsin-Minnesota border. An immigrant German gamekeeper, Burkhart, by all accounts, has been recognized as one of the all-time great GSP breeders. At the time, the breed was not very common and breeders were extremely scarce.

"I soon realized that a dog would be very helpful in census work, since we had four types of game birds on the area," said Art. "Sam thought that a German pointer would be a good all-around dog for my purposed, so I contacted Burkhart.

"He had a dog trained on [prairie] chickens with a good bloodline, which he would sell for fifty dollars," and according to Art, "that was a lot of money in those days. I was receiving sixty dollars per month from Aldo's lean budget."

As it turned out, the dog with "a good bloodline" was Gotz Vom Tuebingen, son of Feldjagers Grisette and Klaus Vom Schwarenberg, universally recognized as significant imports with profound effects on the future of the breed in America. Gus, translated from his registered name, Gotz, was later bred at least twice and prodiced Vicki Vom Schwarenberg, who in turn produced Rusty Vom Schwarenberg. Rusty went on to become a legend as the first GSP Dual Champion in 1947. In becoming the first dual, he is now recognized as winning the fires-ever American Kennel Club (AKC) Field Trial Championship.

Art didn't know it at the time, but his "census dog" and hunting companion, Gus, would eventually become even more famous than his grandson, Rusty.

In a recent interview Art recalled, "I gave Gus to Aldo Leopold in 1938 when I moved to a job with the Illinois Natural History Survey with no way to keep a dog. Gus must have measured up to Aldo's standards because on January 20, 1944, he wrote to Burkhart as follows: 'Gus turned out to be one of the most brilliant field dogs I ever owned.'"

When Art gave his dog to Leopold, he felt it was the best gift he could think of to show his appreciation to the professor for all he had done. Years later, it occurred to him that in so doing, his present may have created problems for the professor.

"Gus was not a city dog. My leaving moved him from the country into a densely populated city – Madison. Maybe the Leopold family wasn't happy to have Gus, at least at first."

I recently asked Nina Leopold Bradley, one of Aldo Leopold's daughters, about her recollections of Gus and their second GSP Flick.

"I'm delighted at your interest in our great dogs, Gus and Flick. They were, indeed, major parts of the Leopold family," she wrote. "One recollection of Gus is that between weekends at the Shack, Gus built up a great deal of energy, as he was confined to the city. Sometimes when he was let out before bedtime, he would take off, resulting in midnight telephone calls, usually from some tavern on the east side of Madison, saying, "Professor, your dog is here at my tavern, would you please come and pick him up?" You can imagine the next happening - Dad, dressing, driving, swearing, gathering up the dog."

Aldo Leopold, now widely recognized as the father of wildlife management, was more than a hunter that opening day back in 1936. According to those who knew him well, hunting was a learning experience and his pathway into a world few others understood.

Leopold shared his outdoor experiences with us all in *A Sand*

County Almanac, recognized worldwide as a conservation classic. As far as I can tell, no single person, place, or subject is mentioned more often in the Almanac than Gus. Here's an example:

"The dog, when he approaches the briars, looks around to make sure I am within gunshot... He is the prospector of the air, perpetually searching its strata for olfactory gold. Partridge scent is the gold standard that related his world to mine."

Leopold, the professor, became the student when following Gus in the sand counties of central Wisconsin. While immersed in observing the natural world along the trail, the dog's eyes and nose instructed the hunter. I'm convinced the dogs that preceded and followed Gus brought this great conservationist and philosopher closer to the land. Again from the Almanac:

"My dog, by the way, thinks I have much to learn about partridges, and, being a professional naturalist, I agree. He persists in tutoring me, with the calm patience of a professor of logic, in the art of drawing deductions from and educated nose. I delight in seeing him deduce a conclusion, in the form of a point, from data that are obvious to him, but speculative to my unaided eye. Perhaps he hopes his dull pupil will someday learn to smell."

From childhood on, Leopold was seldom without a dog at his side. His father Carl was a hunter of great reputation and, according to student Robert A. McCabe, taught his children ethics of chase and value of wildlife. Said McCabe, "A.L. and his brothers were schooled in hunting behavior, restraint, moderation, and subtlety, a reverence for the species hunted."

Archived pictures show young Aldo, at three years of age,

with a springer spaniel named Flick. A few years later, he followed the family dog into the woods carrying a single-shot shotgun and his father's words ringing in his ears, warning him against shooting birds from trees. Leopold wrote:

"My dog was good at treeing partridge and to forego a sure shot in the tree in favor of a hopeless one at the fleeing bird was my first exercise in ethical codes…. I could draw a map today of each clump of red bunchberry and each blue aster that adorned the mossy spot where he lay, my first partridge on the wing. I suspect my present affection for bunchberries and asters dates back to the day."

My research revealed that from 1890 to 1948, Leopold had at least nine dogs, four of whom were named Flick. The nine included three spaniels; two setters; an Irish terrier; a collie; and the last two, Gus and Flick, were German shorthaired pointers.

In late 1943, Art Hawkins, who at the time was serving in the military in Texas, received a copy of a manuscript, *Gus's Last Hunt* from Leopold, later published in Leopold's book *Round River*.

But it's that opening day back in 1936 that still brings back fond memories to Art. He wanted to show off his census dog to his boss, but recalls it as one of his most embarrassing moments.

"He disappeared as though on the trail of a pheasant, but soon reappeared, a squealing piglet in his mouth." Ultimately, as Art recalls, "Gus redeemed himself before the day was over."

Indeed, he did. And ultimately, Gus went on to contribute to the foundation stock of his breed in the United States, and his extraordinary relationship with Aldo Leopold certainly contributed in bring the world closer to the land.

3

BUILDING ON LEOPOLD'S LEGACY

On October 7, 1999 Art Hawkins, at age 85, shared the stage with a distinguished panel that included such dignitaries as Larry Jahn, Estella Leopold, Gaylord Nelson and Lynn Greenwalt. He was participating in a Wisconsin Academy of Arts sponsored conference in Madison, Wisconsin – entitled "Building on Leopold's Legacy – Conservation for a New Century". This is a portion of Art's presentation during the "Speaking with our Elders" segment and sets the stage for our look at his lifetime passion for conservation ethics.

"Next month marks the sixty-fifth anniversary of my first contact with Aldo Leopold, a contact which changed the direction of my life. I was a grad student at Cornell when I learned of an opening under Leopold at the University of Wisconsin. He and I exchanged letters and much to my surprise, I was accepted as his third graduate student. Until noon we exchanged experiences and he briefed me on my new assignment as his research assistant, for which I would receive $30 a month and travel expenses. During those depression years, that sounded great! At noon, we walked a mile to the house for lunch, where I met Mrs. Leopold and their daughters Nina and Estella. Thus began my new career. From that day forward, Aldo became my teacher, mentor and close friend until he died fourteen years later. During the last three years of his life he shared his office space with me in the limited confines of Dean Russell's former home at 424 University Farm Place on this Wisconsin campus. At the time I was a flyaway biologist for the Fish and Wildlife Service, and he provided this office space and some stenographic services at no cost to the government. In partial exchange, I provided some classroom help and served as an advisor to some of his grad students.

The text of my presentation at this workshop is taken from Leopold's book, Game Management, published in 1933 - and I quote: "In short, twenty centuries of progress have brought the average citizen a vote, a national anthem, a Ford, a bank account, and a high opinion of himself; but not the capacity to live in high density without befouling and denuding his environment, nor conviction that such capacity, rather than such density, is the true test of whether he is civilized." We, this panel of old timers and you, the audience of conservationists, are challenged here today to assess the progress made since Leopold's time toward living in an even higher density without befouling or denuding our environment. How well have we conservationists identified the unresolved dangers to our planet and to ourselves, and how well are we prepared to cope with them? Conservation's goal, according to Leopold, is to achieve a state of harmony between land and man. He knew that reaching such a goal would take a long time for he wrote, "Despite nearly a century of propaganda, conservation still moves at a snail's pace. Progress still consists largely of letterhead pieties and conventionality, but on the back forty we still slip two steps backward for each forward stride." I think that statement applies equally well today. Sure, we can list many outstanding achievements in conservation since Leopold's time but just as many failures. In the arena with which I was most familiar, wildlife management for example, I can point out to all the attention given to migratory birds resulting in the massive refuge program, international treaties, and the North American Management Plan for Waterfowl. But counteracting these achievements to a large extent, have been drainage, factory farming, urbanization, pollution, and other negative factors. This being the case, how can the ultimate goal of sustainability ever be achieved? Leopold asked himself a similar question in the search for the truth, and also answered it. One of my favorite quotations from Leopold: "There must be some force behind conservation more universal than profit, less awkward than government, less ephemeral than sport; something that reaches into all time and places where men live on land; something that brackets everything, from rivers to raindrops, from whales to hummingbirds, from land estates to window boxes." He continues, "I can see only one such force; a respect for the land as an organism, a voluntary decency in land use exercised by every citizen and every landowner, out of a sense of love and obligation to that great biota we call America. This is the meaning of conservation, and this is the task of conservation education." But then he raises a question: "Do conservation educators possess the knowledge and skills necessary to serve as qualified spokes people?" He wrote, "The usual answer to this dilemma is more conservation education. No one will debate this, but is it certain that the volume of education needs stepping up, or, is something lacking in the content itself?" He might have added, if the volume and content now exist in proper proportions, how come so little progress has been made toward broadening conservation's base.

Surely we have more knowledge and more tools available to educators than Leopold had - TV and computers, to name two such tools. But polls show that many Americans still consider evolution to be a non-proven theory, showing that education sometimes falls on deaf ears. Somewhere along the line, conservation has come highly politicized, with people choosing one side or the other, with little regard to the central issue. Conservationists have acquired names with bad connotations: eco freaks, tree huggers, human boomers, animal lovers, or even worse, brought on by the extremists among us. Even so, opinion polls seem to show that the majority of Americans claim to be conservationists at heart. But many of them are fair-weather friends at best, with only a shallow understanding of what conservation and land ethic mean. Whose fault is that? And how can the extremists and non-believers be made to realize that conservation is not an economics versus ecology, but rather a blending of the two, and that our survival and well-being depends on both of them?

I agree with Leopold that the only hope for the future of this planet lies in an effective conservation education program based on a universally adopted land ethic. Reaching this level of civilization may be a lot more difficult than even Leopold envisioned. Add to the population density, the vision of the rewards of the better life advertised by the television and broadcast all over the world, and the problem of conversion becomes really complicated. How can conservation and conservation education be brought to the forefront of public discourse and action? First, the public must receive, as Leopold pointed out, and I quote, "a system of conservation based solely on economic self-interest is hopelessly lopsided. It tends to ignore and is eventually to eliminate many elements in the land community that lack commercial value." He goes on to say, "The key log that must be removed to release the evolutionary process is simply this: Quit thinking about decent land use as solely an economic problem. Examine each question in terms of what is ethically and aesthetically right as well as what is economically expedient. It of course goes without saying that economic feasibility limits the tether of what can or cannot be done on the land. The fallacy the economic extremists have tied around our collective neck, and which we now need to cast off, is the belief that economics determines all land use.

"Today, as I see it, economics does in fact determine most land use. If so, the question is how do we cast off this defining yoke? Money and growth are the current yardsticks of progress, and technology is the pat answer to all our woes. But this is a finite world, and growth cannot go on forever. What will technology do when the wells and products of the land run dry? Economists and conservationists must explore these questions together in good faith in the best interests of all humanity. History tells us that attaining significant change in conservation matters is a slow process which grows from the grass roots up, not from the government down. The seeds are sown in conservation nurseries, but it takes educators to bring the crop to maturity." That's the way Aldo Leopold saw it a half century ago, and that's the way it is still today.

4

BATAVIA (1913)

A rthur S. Hawkins was born on June 15, 1913, in Batavia, New York. Son of Olive Ann Prescott and John Arthur Hawkins. Batavia is a city in western New York, near the center of Genesee County. The city's name is Latin for the Betuwe region of the Netherlands, a name which honors early Dutch settlers. Art's parents immigrated from England in the late 1800s. His father was a machinist for Massey-Harris Harvester Company and his mother was, in Art's own words, "just a housewife." The following is his account of his life in Batavia:

I lived in a small town that had quick access to the country. As a matter of fact, it was only two or three blocks away from where we lived, so it was almost like living out in the country, but not quite. My cruising radius was limited to how far I could get with a bike, or on foot, and still meet such obligations as going to school and running my paper route. We never owned a car in my family. We never really needed one. My dad could walk to work, and shopping was easily done in those days with, in our case, three or four groceries within easy walking distance. We could also order, and have them delivered, free of charge. The milkman delivered to the house, and so did the iceman.

My father came from England at age eight. He was good at athletics. He played semi-pro baseball. He never hunted, and only fished once or twice to my knowledge. My mother grew up in a rural atmosphere, but without hunters in the family. My grandfather had hunted some in England, possibly as a poacher, and he gave me my first gun. It was a single-barrel, Lefevre, twelve-gauge hammerless. My first game shot, as I recall, was a woodcock. By then I had a English pointer named "Pep". Together, one evening, we went hunting in a patch of aspens and hawthorns, after one of my newspaper customers told me about seeing some strange looking long-billed birds behind of their place. I recall shooting my first woodcock with a 30-inch, full choke, twelve-gauge gun using number four shot, which of course isn't exactly what is recommended. Another customer, named Fannie Brunson was a typical little old lady in tennis shoes, and whenever I stopped to collect for the newspaper she would show me pictures from the Reed's Bird Guide. I then bought a copy. One Sunday that must have been in May I went for a hike, and stumbled into a wave of migrating warblers. By then my Mother had given me a pair of "two power" opera glasses. It was really an awakening to me, to see this array of warblers, and identifying them, one by one, in my bird book. I have been a "birder" ever since. Meanwhile, I went fishing and camping at every opportunity. The place where we did most of our fishing was about five miles away. We would pedal out there on our bicycles almost every evening. We went to a place called "Godfrey's Pond". As a matter of fact, after school was out, Ernie Haus and I put a tent there, and had it there all summer. We didn't have to worry so much about people stealing things in those days. In the fall, I ran a trap-line before school. During Christmas vacation my first year at Cornell (1931), I trapped muskrats with Arnold Keller. He was a taxidermist and a hunter, fisher and trapper sharing some of his skills with me. One of the most memorable school days I can recall was the day that the school closed during an ice storm. Arnold called to say that he and Mark Salway, the local game warden, were going out to feed the pheasants, and "would you like to join us?" "Would I, you bet I would!" We threw food, shelled corn, along some county roads for the pheasants because their food plants were covered with ice.

5

CORNELL UNIVERSITY (1930)

A rt graduated from Batavia High School in 1930. That fall he walked 50 miles to Cornell, New York and enrolled as an undergraduate in the school of forestry and later in field biology at the University. He graduated from Cornell in 1934. It turned out to be a critical component of his path to meeting Aldo Leopold.

"When the time came to go to college, I enrolled at Cornell University's Forestry School, which was closest to where my interest lay, and the tuition was free. In those days there was no game management program, or anything approaching it, except what you could pick up incidentally in Biology. At the end of my second year at Cornell, the Forestry School was moved to Syracuse, and by then, I was aware that Cornell had perhaps the strongest teaching staff in the country in courses of field biology, so I changed to that curriculum. This was perhaps the wisest decision ever made by me up to that time. It opened the door that lead to Wisconsin and to Aldo Leopold. Cornell provided some unique opportunities beyond course work. Under the NYA program, which was the National Youth Administration during the 1930s, I worked under Dr. Bill Hamilton on various mammal projects, for which I was paid fifty cents per hour.

"On weekend and holidays, I worked on a major grouse research project, based at Connecticut Hill, which is near Ithaca. The summer after graduation in 1934, I had my first real job, with the New York state Conservation Department, working in a lake and stream survey of the Mohawk-Hudson watershed. The summer before, I had helped conduct a biological survey of the Tionesta forest in Pennsylvania. My big moment came in November of 1934 after I had returned to Cornell to work on my "MS" under Dr. Embody, in fisheries.

"One day, another advisor, Dr. Arthur Allen, called me into his office. He had just received a letter from a new professor of game management at the University of Wisconsin named Aldo Leopold. He asked if Dr. Allen had a student who would be interested in conducting a quail study. The quail population had spread, over the past two or three years, in Wisconsin, way outside of its usual range, sometimes called irruption, due to a series of mild winters. He needed a graduate student who could follow some sample populations and see what happened. He would provide a handsome stipend of sixty dollars a month for me, with travel, as I pursued an advanced degree. Times were hard in the 1930s, and I was running low on funds, so the proposal sounded good, and I applied for the job. Leopold asked for one of my publications, but at the time, I had none, so I sent him a term paper on the general subject of conservation, in my handwriting. Professor Leopold must have been in a real bind for a student, because he accepted me. I loaded up my second hand Ford Model A Coupe, with all of my worldly possessions, and right after Christmas, headed west over the narrow icy roads, arriving in Madison on New Year's Day of 1935."

6

WISCONSIN (1935)

Art left his family in New York right after Christmas 1934, arriving in in Madison, Wisconsin on New Year's Day 1935 after being accepted by Professor Aldo Leopold as his third graduate student in the University's new Department of Game Management. Art was to conduct a Bobwhite quail field study in southwestern Wisconsin. This he would later describe as "perhaps the wisest decision ever made by me up to that time. It opened the door that lead to Wisconsin and to Aldo Leopold."

"I was taken in by the Emlins, the only people I knew out there. John Emlin and I had roomed together at Cornell the spring before. He had taken his PhD., married that June, and moved to Madison to work with Leopold on a government program dealing with sub-marginal lands. Johnny was based at the New Soils building where Leopold was based. The next morning he directed me to Leopold's office, where I met Vivian Horn, Leopold's secretary.

"Promptly at 8:30 Leopold's office door opened and I met my new boss, who welcomed me into his office as if I were some dignitary. His desk was clear, and he left instructions with Miss Horn, not to be interrupted. He outlined the quail situation, and what he hoped to learn about it. I am sure that he learned a lot about me from my answers to his questions, put in such an informal and friendly way. At noon, he insisted that I go home with him to lunch, and to meet some of his family. I expected to go outside and jump into the car. But instead, we walked a mile to his house, as was his practice.

"After lunch, he excused himself for a short nap, while I chatted with Mrs. Leopold, and their daughters, Nina and Estella. We walked back to the office where I was dismissed to get ready to start my fieldwork, because time was wasting. This all happened on January 2, 1935, and it made a tremendous impression on me. This impression never changed with respect to how friendly Leopold was to people he met regardless of their status.

"Ten days after our meeting Leopold had his 48th birthday. He took the next day off to visit his friend Ed Ochsner at Prairie du Sac and together they took a drive along some rural roads familiar to Ed. They spotted a worn out farm with only a chicken house still standing, and before long it became known as 'the Shack,' now known as the Mecca for conservationists, worldwide.

"I established five quail study areas that winter. One of them was in Coon Valley, in southwestern Wisconsin, which was the first Soil Erosion Service demonstration area in the country. This project combined forestry, agriculture practices and wildlife management. My northernmost study area, the upper fringe of the quail range at that time, was based at Babcock, near a C.C.C. [Civilian Conservation Corps] camp in central Wisconsin. The other three areas that I chose to work on quail were closer to Madison. One of them was Paul Errington's quail study area at Prairie du Sac. Riley, and Faville Grove, both near Madison, were the other two areas.

"I spent one of the early weeks after I arrived in Wisconsin working with Franklin Schmidt. We worked on banding prairie chickens near where the Hammerstroms later set up their long-term prairie chicken study. Before we got well into the study however, weather conditions ended the quail irruption, and my assignment changed. Professor Leopold decided that I could better spend my time becoming manager of the Faville Grove Wildlife Experimental Station, a training ground for new Leopold students, some of whom, including me, conducted their research there."

In 1938 Art took a position with the Illinois Natural History Survey then in 1941 served in the military during WWII before returning to Madison to work for Professor Leopold once more.

"When I got out of the military, Leopold insisted that I share his very limited office space at 424 University 7 Farm Place, the building in which his whole department was housed. He didn't charge the government anything for having me housed there. My part there was to help out with some of the students. I participated in seminars and also worked with some of the grad students who were going into the waterfowl field. At times when he was called out of town unexpectedly, I took over some of his classes for him. I had three years with Leopold before he finally died."

7

FAVILLE GROVE (1935)
A PRAIRIE ROMANCE

On March 8, 2000 Art Hawkins made a presentation at the National Conservation Training Center called, "The Leopold Legacy: Sustaining the Momentum. He recalled the historical beginnings of this now famous prairie remnant in southern Wisconsin.

"Faville Grove is the place where several brothers named Faville homesteaded, traveling from Herkimer County in New York by way of the Erie barge canal, walking across Michigan, finally ending up in southeastern Wisconsin, farming several hundred acres. The Favilles donated land for a one-room schoolhouse, and established a creamery beside the school. Alpheum Faville's home became known as Faville Homestead, the buildings nestled on a mature oak savanna. Stoughton Faville was born there in 1852. He was 83 when I first met him, and he lived to be almost 99."

In May of 2014, I interviewed Betty Hawkins at her Hugo, MN home on Lake Amelia. We visited over the course of two inspiring and lovely days about Art and their life together – beginning at Faville Grove where she met Art while she was still attending senior high school at nearby Lake Mills in 1935. During the interview she recalled:

"In the 1840s the Faville brothers walked to Wisconsin from New York and homesteaded in the Crawfish Prairie where I was born. My grandfather was Stoughton Faville. My mother was Ellen Elizabeth Faville. My father was Frank Waite Tillotson. I was born on the prairie and married on the prairie. Art and I were married on July 26, 1941 on the prairie.

"There were 10 farmers, my grandfather, Ben Berg, Krump and others with about 2,000 acres –which made up the Faville Grove wildlife management area. Art and Professor Leopold were popular with farmers eager to have grad students live and work with them. My father graduated from UW- Madison. Art, Bob McCabe and another graduate student named Sowles lived in a second, smaller house grandfather built for himself, but never lived in it. It was not insulated. Besides housing, mother provided the boys meals and did their wash for $27 a month.

"Art had a dog named "Gus". Mom would mix middlings with eggs and milk, bake it into cakes and break off parts. There was a laundry room outside of house for Gus where she fed him and made a bed of straw to make it cozy.

"Everyone liked Art.

"I remember Aldo Leopold would hang around the farm and help with the milking. He was so likeable, with good manners and oh, so polite. My grandfather had a large collection of Indian relics that he had on display – arrowheads and spearheads. He was also proud of his wildflower garden that he and the professor would look at when at the farm. Art and Leopold would eat dinner with our family at times. One time there was 10 people to feed and only one duck. Mr. Leopold had a way to stretch the meat by carefully cutting very thin slices!"

At the Annual Leopold Education project (LEP) National Workshop at Baraboo, WI in August of 2001 Art gave a keynote presentation, "Faville Prairie: Remembering Aldo Leopold", at a field trip to the prairie. The following are excerpts of his talk;

"What a beautiful morning for a field trip! I invite you to join me on a trip down memory lane through Leopold country along paths that my professor and I traveled together 65 years ago. We'll spend most our time at Faville Grove...Our main focus will be on prairies, particularly the Crawfish Prairie at Faville Grove and on how hard Professor Leopold worked to save this prairie from destruction. Then, to top things off, we'll return to Faville Grove and the Crawfish Prairie 65 years later to see what has happened there in recent years.

"On June 26, 1933, Aldo Leopold became the first Professor of Game Management in the country, at a salary of $8,000 per year. That included travel and other expenses of his new office in the Department of Agricultural Economics at the University of Wisconsin (Madison).

"Leopold began his new job as Professor full speed ahead. He quickly became involved in several of (President Roosevelt's) New Deal land management programs, including, that of the Soil Erosion Service (SES) at Coon Valley, Wisconsin, the first project of its kind in the country. Two of Leopold's sons, Starker and Luna, worked on that project, and in 1935 it was one of my quail study areas. Leopold, by then a recognized conservation leader in great demand nationally, turned down lucrative offers in the new Administration to remain in Wisconsin.

"On July 26, 1941, I was in training in the Veterinary Service at Camp Grant, Ill, some 70 miles from Faville Grove. At noon that day, another trainee named John M. (Frosty) Anderson and I waited at the post gate for Betty Tillotson, who had worked that morning at the Creamery Package Co. In Lake Mills. She picked us up in my car, whizzed us back to Faville Homestead where relatives had gathered and we all drove out to Faville Prairie where Betty and I were married amidst the liatris and cone flowers. Betty was Stoughton Faville's grand daughter and that's how I officially joined the Faville clan.

"In 1999 Betty and I returned to Faville grove to help the family celebrate "prairie day" as we called it. During the festivities Betty and I had our picture taken near the spot where we were married 58 years earlier. We visited several new prairie restorations by neighbors Dave Musolf and Roger Pachard already carpeted with prairie flowers which had been row crop or hay field when Leopold last saw them. Three months later after the massive convention at Madison to commemorate the publication of Leopold's "A Sand County Almanac", several of us visited the site of the major new prairie restoration abutting the Stoughton Faville Prairie. Betty's brother Dave and his wife, Frances had recently sold this 50-acre field to Madison Audubon. Later that month volunteer workers from Madison Audubon prepared the field and planted prairie seeds.

"On May 29 of this year, Betty and I returned to Faville Grove for the dedication of "Tillotson Prairie" named by Madison Audubon for its previous owners. The July issue of CAWS, the newsletter of Madison Audubon, tells all about this special event. Help yourself to a copy on the table. To me, this education was an off-shoot of the legacies of pioneers in prairie preservation and restoration, especially Aldo Leopold, Stoughton Faville, John Curtis, Max Patch and Bob McCabe. The seeds they planted 60 years ago are now bearing fruit. Thanks to them and present-day partnership programs, prairie restoration is alive and spreading in the Faville Grove area."

Art Hawkins and his wife, Betty
(photo by Ed Pembleton)

8

FAVILLE GROVE (1935-1937)

At the 6th Annual Leopold Education Project (LEP) National Workshop in August of 2001, Art's keynote presentation was Faville Prairie: Remembering Aldo Leopold. Art recalled his start at the Faville Grove study area.

"In the spring of 1935, I moved from Madison to Faville Grove to become its first wildlife manager, and to work on research projects toward my degree. Dr. Robert A. McCabe, in his report "The Stoughton Faville Prairie Preserve: Some Historical Aspects" quotes from a letter Leopold wrote in 1936 to Professor McNall, of the Ag Economics department: '...think the Faville Grove and Lake Mills community would be an excellent place to make a really serious test of connecting people with the land. And I'm beginning to realize that the extraordinary personality of Stoughton Faville offers a valuable focal point which would help greatly to get the community started in this direction.'

"McCabe points out that this 2,000-acre study area was used from 1935-1941 as a training area for University grad students in Wildlife Management. At least ten students were stationed at Faville Grove, and received training or completed research on the area. McCabe was the last of the full-time students to be part of this area-oriented research program before World War II intervened.

"I was Professor Leopold's first student to receive an advanced degree. After having received my Master's degree in 1937, I moved to Illinois as a member of the Illinois Natural History Survey, but under agreement that I could return to Wisconsin at intervals to complete unfinished projects.

"As the clouds of World War II thickened, demands on agricultural production increased, and one early casualty was the Crawfish Prairie at Faville Grove. Two local people, one a high school ag teacher, the other a banker, decided that with a few ditches, the Crawfish Prairie offered a great place to grow corn. In a remarkably short time, the Crawfish Prairie, one of the best virgin wet prairies in the state, was converted to farmland, except for one parcel of about 60 acres, saved mainly through the efforts of Leopold and his friends, Mr. and Mrs. Philip Miles, who purchased the property. The prairie relec was named "The Stoughton Faville Prairie Preserve", in honor of the patriarch of Faville Grove.

"In his paper, McCabe goes into great detail about Leopold's attempts to save the best parts of the Crawfish Prairie. According to McCabe, in October 1938, "Aldo Leopold had in his hands a fair land value of $17.50 per acre for Crawfish Prairie Land". Despite the favorable combination of a willing seller, whose lawyer also favored the deal, and a more than willing buyer, no one could come up with the cash to close the deal, in that Depression period. The seller, needing the cash, became impatient with the slow progress of the negotiations, and on May 15, 1940, moved his cattle onto the choicest part of the prairie, which included the booming ground of the fast-disappearing prairie chickens. On May 12, 1941, I came back to Faville Grove for a brief visit. During my stay, Aldo Leopold, Bob McCabe and I dug up clumps of about 50 small white lady slippers and using an old door as a litter, moved them to a safer place. The success of this transplant was affirmed this spring by Chuck Johannsen, a photographer, who wrote; "I'd like to thank you for transplanting those white lady slippers to the northwest corner of Faville Prairie…(Leopold's) essay Exit Orchis evidently was written in response to the situation Professor Leopold described. Anyway, the orchids are doing great. I've never seen so any orchids in one place. That northwest corner was carpeted with them."

On June 29, 1936, Art sent a letter to the Editor to Jefferson County area newspapers. The following is the letter and how the news article appeared:

Faville Grove Wildlife Area
Lake Mills, Wisconsin
June 29, 1936
To the editors of the Jefferson County newspapers:

The University of Wisconsin, Department of Wildlife Management, has undertaken an intensive nesting survey in Jefferson county. In addition to a small crew of field workers, this survey is being aided by the Land Economic Survey, which is just starting in this county, and by the county 4-H clubs, as well as road crews, creameries, and other agencies.
The success of the nesting study depends on the individual

farmer of this county. All we ask is that each farmer will jot down, on the form sheet which we are distributing, the kind of game bird nest he finds, whether it is in a hay field, fence row, etc., and the date on which he finds it. Since this study is especially interested in determining the hay field mortality of the hungarian partridge, we would also like to know the hay acreage on which the farmers nesting observations were made, and the dates on which the hay was cut, so that we can determine how much the hay fields are used by nesting game birds at different times during the summer. Of course, any additional observations made by the farmers will be very welcome, and space is left on the nesting blank for additional information.

We would greatly appreciate the cooperation of your paper in reaching the farmers of your section.

The nesting reports can be sent to my office at Faville Grove, telephoned in, (number 3776), or given to any 4-H club leader.

We would appreciate it if your office could also be listed as a receiving station for the nesting reports.

Sincerely yours,

Arthur S. Hawkins, Manager

A University nesting survey followed asking cooperation of all Jefferson County farmers.

"The University of Wisconsin Department of Wildlife Management has undertaken an intensive nesting survey in Jefferson county. A.S. Hawkins, manager of the Faville Grove Wildlife area, is directing the survey in an attempt to determine the nesting mortality among the game birds of the county.

"Six men of the Faville Grove area, sixteen men on the county covery survey, creameries and road mowing crews are attempting to make a complete report on the number of nests broke up during haying and reaping, but they need the assistance of every farmer in this vicinity.

"Nesting questionnaires will be sent to every farmer on which he can fill in the number of nests disturbed, kind of birds, number of eggs location and whether the bird returned after mowing. All game bird nests will be charted but special attention in being paid to Hungarian partridges.

"Farmers are asked to send in a report immediately after the first haying to A.S. Hawkins, Faville Grove Wildlife Area.

"A Century of Agriculture is Jefferson County" is the program being arranged by the centennial committee to be featured on the Dinner Bell program over W.L.S. Tuesday, July 7, Winnebago Indian chanters are scheduled to sing, and A.S. Hawkins, manager of the Faville Grove Wildlife Area, Frank Everson, county agent, will speak."

The following talk was given by Art over radio station WLS on July 7, 1936 to help celebrate "A Century of Agriculture in Jefferson County - Faville Grove Wildlife Area Yesterday, Today, and Tomorrow."

"When the first white settler arrived nearly a century ago, he found that over half of Faville Grove's 2400 acres was open grass prairie interspersed with an occasional bur oak island. The remainder of the area was a mixture of wooded upland and tamarack swamps.

"The clear waters of the Crawfish River, with its plentiful

supply of wild rice and other fine duck foods, added to the charm of the prairie. Fish abounded in this beautiful stream which was also the breeding and feeding ground of countless wildfowl, and water-loving furbearers. Many old timers still alive can remember the vast numbers of prairie chicken living on the Crawfish prairie.

"Deer, ruffed grouse, passenger pigeons, and quail thrived on the plentiful food supply furnished by the park-like oak groves – park-like because the Indians burned these prairie woods annually, and the underbrush could not develop.

'Old timers remember two more or less important wildlife problems affecting their early agriculture; one was the countless numbers of passenger pigeons which made grain planting a real problem, and the other was the sporadic ravages of coyotes on their herds of sheep.

"Wildlife and all nature, during the pioneer days, were an inseparable part of the settler's life. His successes and his failures were both closely linked with wildlife and its environment.

"With this brief account of Faville Grove a century ago, let's bring the picture up to date. It took the early settlers but a short time to realize that the soil was rich and productive. As a result, a land boom followed; and agriculture began in earnest.

"First, the area was given over almost exclusively to wheat growing. Log, rail, and stump fences were built to divide the fields and get rid of the surplus timber.

"Quail, rabbits, passenger pigeons, and even ruffed grouse found this early agriculture quite favorable to their needs, as it gave better interspersion of cover and food types. At the same time, however, certain other species, such as and otter, were forced to retreat before the plow and axe.

"A prosperous dairy industry soon sprang up, and clean farming became the rule. Almost all species of wildlife began to feel the pressure of heavy framing and over-hunting, and become much reduced in numbers, or even exterminated on the area. The once beautiful Crawfish River became muddy, shallow, and without vegetation, thus reducing it to a shadow of its former productivity. This was partly due to silting caused by the cultivation of many new fields, and partly to the work of the newly-introduced carp.

"It happens that at Faville Grove lives a man whose interests in modern farming are so great that he received on of the most coveted awards given by Wisconsin to those farmers obviously leading the way in agriculture. Mr. Stoughton Faville receive this recognition for his pioneering work in holstein breeding.

"Yet in spite of the fact that Mr. Faville had something of a struggle to keep his large farm running smoothly, and to give his four children's college education, he found time for the finer things of life–the appreciation of man and nature. He found time to play an active part in church and community affairs. Still more remarkable, he somehow found time to become the local authority on Indian relics, and to become known to Wisconsin botanists as a leading wildflower, conservationists, and an authority on the orchids of Wisconsin. One orchid had been named for Mr. Faville, who discovered it.

"What more fitting than that the University of Wisconsin should establish a wildlife management demonstration centered around Mr. Faville's farm? Mr. Faville and the other nine farmers of the area want wildlife brought back without a great deal of sacrifice, in time and money, to the land owner. True, game will never be as abundant as it once was. Man's pecuniary instincts forbid that. But with careful management, a respectable wildlife population can once more become a part of the American farm.

"Almost a century has passed since the early pioneer days of this region, but Faville Grove is again pioneering–this time in an attempt to reconnect man with nature in everyday life. The passenger pigeon, deer, otter, and ruffed grouse now only exist in pleasant memories of some of the oldest old timers, and only a remnant of the once abundant prairie chicken is left. To replace the native game bird species which have been exterminated from the area, hungarian partridge and ring-necked pheasant were introduced about ten years ago, and have now become established.

"About three years ago, at the request of the local farmers, the University of Wisconsin, under Professor Aldo Leopold, began to make use of some of the many opportunities to be found on the area, to study the resident wildlife and its relation to the farmer. Incidentally, similar opportunities are present in almost any farming community.

"An attempt is being made to put as many of the findings as seem practical from the standpoint of the land owner, into actual practice.

"It might be well to digress a moment to mention two basic principles which the farmer interested in increasing wildlife should remember: The improvement of winter food and cover conditions is a long step in building up a game crop, while fencing against grazing is the only way to protect most of the choice wild flowers.

"During the past few years, public sentiment toward

conservation – particularly soil conservation – has been growing. Wildlife conservation goes hand in hand with soil conservation. Thus, a system of experimental and demonstration area for wildlife management is developing under federal, state, and local auspices. Faville Grove Wildlife area is part of this system, and as such, is helping to mold the future wildlife history of this vicinity. Perhaps its influence will extend over a much larger area–who can say?"

9

ILLINOIS NATURAL HISTORY SURVEY
& FAVILLE GROVE (1938-1940)

In 1938, Art left Wisconsin to accept a position with the Illinois Natural History Survey and was stationed not far south of the Wisconsin state line in Urbana, Illinois. Aldo and Art exchanged many letters over the course of the next decade, as Art went to Illinois, then Texas - serving the military during the war years - and finally to Manitoba, following his career north as a wildlife biologist. Art saved all the letters from his professor during those years. I found a letter dated May 16, 1938 in Art's files from Aldo Leopold's secretary Vivian Horn, apparently responding to a letter from Art requesting paychecks from his last days employed at the University of Wisconsin.

Dear Art:

Somehow I had a feeling that if I just held on to those checks I would hear from you sooner or later.

I am in rather a hurry at the moment, otherwise I would write you a long, chatty letter telling you <u>everything</u> that has happened since you've been gone. As it is I have to type some things for Mr. Leopold as a result of a conference he had with

Dean Fred at which he pried loose another assistantship–which helps a great deal for the next year.

Sounds as though the time has not been exactly hanging on your hands. If it were not for the mosquitos you mention, I would suggest that perhaps the Survey should provide you with a secretary.

As ever,
Viv

While away from Wisconsin, and for the rest of his life, Faville Grove was never far from Art's thoughts. In Art's Hugo files I found an October 21, 1939 handwritten letter to Art from local farmer-cooperator Joe Hickey* and accompanying note to Aldo from Art.

Aldo:
I ran across this in going thru some old correspondence.

We don't have much to show for our joint efforts at Lake Mills (Faville Grove) but letters like this suggest that maybe we do some good after all.

Thought you might like to see it.
Art

Dear Art

You don't know until you are in the dumps how much a letter like yours can mean to a person. Really I'm like a ship without a rudder nothing in the future to get to. Of course I have a little money but it seems like ambition is gone.

I couldn't think of father or the sons Are giving me they get in my hair and for him he couldn't I rent a place for cash as he is hard-pressed there I hear. you know art I had a lot of fun feeding the birds. What I have done for the area was nothing compared to my pleasure in knowing all of you especially Dr. L. You and Lyle and Aldo owes me nothing except the pleasant memories I have.

I think Aldo and I are going to take Gus out this afternoon. I hope to get one this morning just in case. I got skunked yesterday for the first time... Farmers Island is full of birds but when I get one there it's just plain luck. Monday I didn't intend on going hunting went to the mailbox and there were 3 in the cornfield went to the house and got the gun and made a double. Felt like an expert.

Well so long Art. I don't know where I'm going but may well know where I am.

Yours,

Hickey

I'll surely see you again sometime.

*Note - Joe Hickey, according to Robert A. McCabe, was a pallbearer at the Professor's funeral in Burlington, Iowa on April 23, 1948.

In May of 1940, Aldo Leopold wrote Art and asked him to review an essay he wrote to be used at an upcoming event. The Professor often asked his graduate students to read, edit and comment on his papers. I found many of those requests in Art's files. You may recognize this essay, destine for ultimate notoriety.

EXIT ORCHIS

Wisconsin conservation will suffer a defeat when, at the end of this week, 75 cattle will be turned to pasture on the

Faville Grove Prairie, long known to botanists as one of the largest and best remnants of unplowed, ungrazed prairie sod left in the State. In it grow the white ladyslipper, the white fringed orchis, and some twenty other prairie wildflowers which originally carpeted half of the southern part of the State, but most of which are now rare due to their inability to withstand cow or plow.

Thirty miles away a C.C.C camp on the University of Wisconsin Arboretum has been busy for four years artificially replanting a prairie in order that botany classes and the public generally may know what a prairie looked like, and what the word "prairie" signifies in Wisconsin history. This synthetic prairie is costing the taxpayer twenty times as much as what it would have cost to buy the natural remnant at Faville Grove, it will be only a quarter as large, the ultimate survival of its transplanted wildflowers and grasses is uncertain, and it will always be synthetic. Yet no one has heard the appeals of the University Arboretum Committee for funds to buy the Faville Grove Prairie, together with other remnants of rare native flora, and set them aside as historical and educational reservations. Our educational system is such that white fringed orchis means as little to the modern citizen of Wisconsin as it means to a cow. Indeed it means less, for the cow at least sees something to eat, whereas the citizen sees only three meaningless words.

In preparation for the hoped-for floral reservation at Faville Grove, the Botany Department and the Department of Wildlife Management of the University have, during the last three years, mapped the location of each surviving colony of rare flowers, and each spring have counted the blooms. It was hoped to measure against these data the response of the flowers to complete future protection. The data will now serve to measure the rate at which destruction by grazing takes place. It is already known that with the possible exception of ladies tresses, all the rarer species succumb to pasturing. That is why they are rare. Few of them succumb to mowing, hence the past use of the Faville Grove Prairie as haymeadow has not greatly injured its flora.

In my opinion no individual blame attaches to the owner of the Faville Grove Prairie for converting it to pasture. The public taxes him on the land. It is not his obligation to provide the public with free botanical reservations, especially when all public institutions, from the public school to the federal land bank, urge him to squeeze every possible penny out of every possible acre. No public institution ever told him, or any other farmer, that natural resources not convertible into cash have any value to it or to him. The white-fringed orchis is as irrelevant to the cultural and economic system into which he was born as the Taj Mahal or the Mona Lisa.

John Muir, who grew up amid the prairie flowers in Columbia County, foresaw their impending disappearance from the Wisconsin landscape. In about 1865 he offered to buy from his brother a small part of the meadow of the family homestead, to be fenced and set aside as a floral sanctuary or reservation. His offer was refused. I imagine that his brother feared not so much the loss of a few square rods of pasture as he feared the ridicule of his neighbors.

By 1965, when the rarer prairie flowers are gone, the cultural descendants of John Muir's brother may look at a picture of the legendary white fringed orchis and wish they could see one.

10

MILITARY SERVICE TEXAS &
LETTERS TO/FROM ART (1941-1947)

O
n November 28, 1941 the professor wrote Art the following letter addressed to Camp Grant, Illinois, but forwarded to Lake Mills, Wisconsin. Perhaps during Art's and Betty's time back when they were married on July 26, 1941 at Faville Grove before returning to Texas, where they lived from January of 1942 to October of 1946. The War was on, and according to Betty, they drove a second hand Chevy to Amarillo, Texas where Art, a Sargent, was stationed for 4 years.

Dear Arthur:

Here is a rough draft of the talk you helped me outline. You will notice that I didn't cover more than a fraction of the ground we talked about.

If you have any suggestions, I'd be glad to have them. Mark up this copy and return it if that is the quickest way.

With best regards,

Aldo

Rough Draft
Mid-western W L Conference
December 4, 1941

WILDLIFE IN AMERICAN CULTURE
Aldo Leopold

When we speak of "buffalo Indians", we imply that in primitive people's the entire culture, including not only food-economy, but also architecture, dress, language, and religion may be rooted in some wild animal or plant.

When we speak of outdoor recreation, we imply that in civilized peoples the economic base has shifted to tame animals and plants, but that the cultural base retains part of its wild roots. People go back to the outdoors because that is where they came from.

This paper deals with the cultural values of this wild rootage.

No one can weigh or measure culture, hence I will waste no time trying to. Suffice it to say that by common consent of all thinking people, there are cultural values in outdoor sports, customs, contacts, and experiences. I will further venture the opinion that these values are of three kinds.

First, there is value in any experience which reminds us of our distinctive origins and evolution, i.e., which stimulates our awareness of American history. Such awareness is "nationalism" and its best sense. For lack of any other short name, I will call this the "split-rail value". For example: a boy scout has tanned him a coonskin cap and goes Daniel-Booneing in the willow thicket below the tracks. He is re-enacting American history. He is, to that extent, culturally prepared to face the dark and bloody realities of 1941.

Second, there is a value in any experience which reminds us of our dependency on the soil-plant-animal-man food-chain. Civilization has so cluttered this elemental man-earth relation with gadgets and middle-men that awareness of it is growing dim. We fancy that industry supports us, forgetting what supports industry. In this respect, education, grown into a pleurisy, may die of its own too-much. Time was when education moved towards soil, not away from it. The nursery jingle about bringing home a rabbit skin to wrap the baby bunting in is one of many reminders in folklore that man once hunted to feed and clothe his family.

Thirdly, the conquest of nature by machines has led to much unnecessary destruction of resources. Our tools grow better faster than we do. It is unlikely that economic motives alone will ever teach us to use our new tools gently. The only remedy is to extend our system of ethics from the man-man relation to the man-earth relation (1). Any experience which stimulates this extension of ethics is culturally valuable. Any which has the opposite effect is culturally damaging. Thus we have many bad hunters with good guns. Such a hunter shoots a woodduck, then tramples the bejeweled carcass into the mud, lest he fall foul of the law. Such an experience is not only devoid of cultural values, it is actually damaging to all concerned. No sane person would find anything but minus value in such "sport".

It seems, then, that split-rail and man-earth experiences have zero or plus values, but that ethical experiences may have minus values as well.

*****

This, then, defines roughly three kinds of cultural nutriment available to our outdoor roots. It does not follow that culture is fed. The extraction of value is never automatic; only a healthy culture can feed and grow. Is culture fed by our present forms of outdoor recreation?

The pioneer period gave birth to two ideas which are the very essence of split-rail value in outdoor sports. One is the "go-light" idea, the other the "one-bullet-one-buck" idea. The pioneer went light because he had to. He shot with economy and precision because he lacked the transport, the cash, and the weapons requisite for machine-gun tactics. Let it be clear then, that in their inception, both these ideas were forced on us; we made a virtue of necessity.

In their later evolution, however, they became a code of ethics, a self-imposed limitation on sport. On them is based a distinctively American tradition of self-reliance, hardihood, woodcraft, and marksmanship. These are intangibles, but they are not abstractions. Theodore Roosevelt was a great sportsman, not because he hung up many trophies, but because he expressed this intangible tradition in words any schoolboy could understand. A more subtle and accurate expression is found in the early writings of Stewart Edward White. It is not far amiss to say that such men created cultural value by being aware of it, and by creating a pattern for its growth.

Then came the gadgeteer, euphemistically known as a sporting goods dealer. He has draped the American outdoorsman with an infinity of devices, all offered as aids to self-reliance, hardihood, woodcraft, or marksmanship, but too often functioning as substitutes for them. The overflow from pockets, neck, and belt fills the car-trunk and then the trailer. Each item of outdoor equipment grows lighter and often better, but the aggregate poundage becomes tonnage. The traffic in gadgets adds up to astronomical sums, which are soberly published as representing "the economic value of wildlife". But what of cultural values?

As an end-case consider the duck hunter, sitting in a steel boat behind composition decoys. A put-put has brought him to the blind without exertion on his part. Canned heat stands by to warm his bottom in case of a blow. He talks to the passing flocks on a factory caller, in what he hopes are seductive tones; home lessons from a phonograph record have taught him how. The decoys work, despite the caller; a flock circles in. It must be shot at before it circles twice, for the marsh bristles with other sportsman, similarly accoutred, who might shoot first. He opens up at 70 yards, for his polychoke is set for infinity, and the ads have told him that Super-Z shells, and plenty of them, have a long reach. The flock flares. A couple of cripples scale off to die elsewhere.

Is this sportsman absorbing cultural value? Or is he just feeding minks?

Next time the neighboring blind opens up at 75 yards; how else is a fellow to get some shooting? This is duck-shooting, model 1941. It is typical of all public grounds, and of many clubs. Where is the go-light idea, the one-bullet tradition?

The answer is not a simple one. Roosevelt did not disclaim the modern rifle; White freely used the aluminum pot, the silk tent, dehydrated foods. Somehow they used mechanical aids, in moderation, without being used by them. I do not pretend to know what moderation is, or where the line is between legitimate and illegitimate gadgets.

It seems clear that the origin of gadgets has much to do with their effects. Home-made aids to sport or outdoor life often enhance, rather than destroy, the man-earth drama; he who kills a trout with his own fly has scored two coups, not one. I use many factory-made gadgets myself, but there must be some limit beyond which money-bought aids to sport destroy the cultural value of sport.

*****

Not all sports have degenerated to the same extent as duck-hunting. Defenders of the American tradition still exist. Perhaps the bow-and-arrow movement and the revival of falconry mark the beginnings of a reaction. The net trend, however, is clearly toward more and more mechanization of sport, with a corresponding shrinkage in cultural values, especially split-rail values and ethical restraints.

I have the strong impression that the American sportsman is puzzled; he doesn't understand what is happening to him. Bigger and better gadgets are good for industry; why aren't they good for outdoor recreation? It has not dawned on him that outdoor recreations are essentially atavistic; that their present value is a contrast-value; that excessive mechanization destroys contrast by moving the factory to the woods or the marsh.

The sportsman has no leaders to point out this obvious trend. The sporting press no longer represents sport, it has turned billboard for the gadgeteer. Wildlife administrators are too busy producing something to shoot at to worry about the cultural value of the shooting. Because everyone from Xenophon to Teddy Roosevelt said sport has value, it is assumed that this value must be indestructible. It remains to be seen whether professional wildlife managers will likewise accept this fallacy.

Among non-gunpowder sports, the impact of mechanization has had diverse effects. The modern field glass, camera, and aluminum bird-band has certainly <u>not</u> deteriorated the cultural value of ornithology. Fishing, but for motorized transport, seems less severely affected than hunting. On the other hand, motorized transport has nearly destroyed wilderness travel by leaving only fly-specks of the wilderness to travel in. Fox-hunting with hounds, backwoods style, presents a dramatic instance of partial and perhaps harmless mechanized invasion. This is one of the purest of sports; it has real split-rail flavor; it has man-earth drama of the first water. The fox is deliberately left unshot, hence ethical restraint is also present. But we now follow the chase in Fords! The voice of the Bugle-Anne mingles with the voice of the fliver! However, no one is likely to invent a mechanical fox-hound, nor to screw a polychoke on the hound's nose; indeed I have yet to see a convincing account of what scent is, or how a dog follows it. No one is likely to teach dog-training by phonograph, or by other painless shortcuts. I think the gadgeteer has reached the end of his tether in dogdom.

It is not quite accurate to ascribe all the ills of sports to the inventor. The advertisers invents ideas, and ideas are seldom as honest as physical objects, even though they may be equally useless. One such deserves special mention: the "where to go" department. Knowledge of the whereabouts of good hunting or fishing is a very personal form of property. Perhaps it is like a rod, dog or gun: a thing to be loaned or given as a personal courtesy, or even to be sold man-to-man, as in the guide-sportsman relation. But to hawk it in the marketplace of the sports column as an aid-to-circulation seems to me another matter. To hand it to all and sundry as free public "service" seems to me another matter. Both tend to de-personalize one of the principle elements in hunting skill. I do not know where the line is between legitimate and illegitimate practice; I am convinced, though, that "where-to-go" service has broken all bounds of reason.

*****

Wildlife management is trying to convert hunting from exploitation to cropping. If the conversion takes place, how will it affect cultural values?

Split-rail flavor and free-for-all exploitation are clearly associated. Daniel Boone head scant patience with agricultural cropping, let alone wildlife cropping. Perhaps the stubborn reluctance of the modern one-gallus sportsman to be converted to the cropping idea is an expression of his split-rail inheritance. He does not object to cropping proceedures which leave the land unposted; thus he likes state game farms, despite the growing evidence that they cost much and accomplish little. He dislikes all cropping procedures which involve posting, despite the growing evidence that posting is a prerequisite to real cropping.

Probably crapping is resisted because it is incompatible with one component of the split-rail tradition: free hunting. Mechanization is not resisted, despite its destructive effect on split-rail value and all other values.

Mechanization offers no cultural substitute for the split-rail values it destroys; at least none visible to me. Cropping or management does offer a substitute, which to me has at least equal value: wild husbandry. The act of managing land for wild-life crops has the same value as any other form of farming; it is a reminder of the man-earth relation. Moreover ethical restraints are involved; thus managing game without resorting to predator-control calls for ethical restraint of a high order. It may be concluded, then, that management shrinks one value (split-rail) but enhances both others.

*****

If we regard outdoor sports as a field of conflict between an immensely vigorous process of mechanization and a wholly static tradition, then the outlook for cultural values is indeed dark. But why can't our concept of sport grow with the same vigor as our list of gadgets? Perhaps the salvation of cultural value lies in seizing the offensive. I, for one, believe that the materials are at hand. With them, we can determine the shape of things to come.

The last decade, for example, has disclosed a totally new form of sport which does not destroy wildlife, which uses gadgets without being used by them, which outflanks the problem of posted land, and which greatly increases the human carrying capacity of a unit area. This sport knows no bag limit, no closed season. It needs teachers, but not wardens. It calls for a new woodcraft of the highest cultural value. The sport I referred to as wildlife research.

Research started as a professional priestcraft, and the more difficult or laborious problems must remain in professional hands. In the mechanical field, research has long since spread to amateurs. In the biological field the sport-value of amateur work is just beginning to be realized. When amateurs like Margaret Nice outstrip their professional colleagues, a very important element is added: high stakes open to all comers the possibility of really outstanding performance.

Ornithology, mammalogy, and botany, is now known to most amateurs, are but rudimentary kindergarten games. The real game is decoding the message written on the face of the land. By learning how some small part of the biota ticks, we can guess how the whole mechanism ticks.

Few people can enthuse about research sports because the whole structure of biological education is aimed to perpetuate the professional monopoly on all but make-believe voyages of discovery. Conservation education is of little avail because it is superimposed on the old base. A new base is needed. If you are a pessimist, you can say it is "on order"; if an optimist, you can see the keel.

In my opinion, the promotion of wildlife research sports is a more important job for our profession than the production of gun-fodder. The gun will never disappear from the picture; it will, I hope, cease to be the sole tool of the hunter.

At the end of Leopold's draft essay he wrote a note to Art;

It was clear after during the speeches at Milwaukee that the previous draft would not ring the bell with the directors hence I took the liberty of revising again, but specifying that no one had signed yet. If the new draft is for any reason not ok with you, let me know.
A.L.

The next month, on January 20, 1942, Aldo wrote to Art once again:

Dear Arthur,
I was glad to get your letter and have delayed reply until I could get to Faville Grove. Feeding may have been faulty during the storm, but I found everything shipshape since then. The census indicates pheasants are way up: 212 birds as compared with 137 last year, but this was not a drive. Both Hungarians

and quail are down, with censuses of 120 and 75 respectively. Arboretum pheasants are up. The drive showed 317 as compared with 299 last year.

I hope you have seen Pete Henika by this time, and I hope you find time to let him show you around, particularly to show you the kites on the Canadian River.

I had a nice visit with the folks at Faville Grove and found Elizabeth looking well and Mr. Faville looking better than usual.

I hadn't seen the Scheinfeld book, but I'm asking Alice to get it for me. Am reading Peattie's "Road of a Naturalist", but find it pretty highly colored.

Most of my time nowadays is spent grinding away at manuscripts–Delta Bulletin, my paper on Prairie du Sac with Paul Errington, and Arboretum pheasants. Fortunately the last is finished. Bob McCabe is making good headway on the Faville Grove Hungarian paper, and I think you will be pleased. He has not started actually writing yet, but has drawings, graphs, and tables finished.

Carl is enlisting in one of the meteorology schools next month.

Please excuse this typewritten reply, but I didn't want to delay longer.

Write me again when you have time.

Yours as ever,

Aldo

P.S. As to the feeding, about forgot this. I have already turned Riley over to the farmers to feed for lack of reliable tires on our students cars. Tires are going to force me to abandon truck work.

Nine days later on January 29th, 1942, the Professor wrote:

Dear Arthur:

Bob is approaching the stage in the Hungarian paper at which the details of writing must be planned. He gave the material at seminar the other evening, and you will be pleased to know that it went over big.

What I would like to ask you is whether Ted Frison expected to have the publication of this paper under his auspices. I am, of course, perfectly willing that it be published by Illinois, and so is Bob, but before saying anything to Ted Frison on the subject, I thought I had better get your impression. If it is to be handled by Illinois, Bob and I need some advance notion of length, style, limitations to plates, etc.

With best regards,
Aldo

That particular letter was addressed to:
Mr. Arthur S. Hawkins
Detachment Medical Department
Station Hospital, building 1268
Sheppard Field, Texas

The next letter from the Professor I found in Art's files was dated October 30, 1942 and addressed to:
Corporal Arthur Hawkins
4235 W. 10th
Amarillo, Texas

Dear Art:

I am much pleased that you like the Amarillo Plains, and especially that you have a sympathetic local friend who is helping you get around.

It's also good news that you have a fairly agreeable assignment now from the Army.

We held the Faville Grove meeting a couple of weeks ago, and I am sending you an extra copy of the shooting rules.

There are lots of pheasants this year everywhere. I got two nice cocks, shooting on the upland of the Farmers' Island on the opening Sunday. Cocks seem to be gathered on the island as a result of the shooting, and most of the hunters were wearing themselves out down in the cattails and tamaracks without seeing many birds. In the thicket on the hill these cocks furnished shooting much like ruffed grouse shooting except, of course, they were considerably slower. Bob McCabe also got a cock in the same place, and we found a fourth one lying dead, apparently a head shot from some distant spot.

Farmers' Island is now full of maidenhair fern. This is, of course, in keeping with your theory that it represents mixed hardwood, but I can't remember their being there in former years, can you?

My brother Carl and I had a very fair grouse hunt from the shack, working the streams in Adams County. The flushing rate was better than either '41 or '40, and about equal to '39. This was a pleasant surprise. The rates were: 1939–4.2 per hour, 1940–3.0 per hour, 1941–3.0 per hour, 1942–4.0 per hour.

Farther north, there are said to be many localities which have already lost their grouse. This would sound like a cycle, but there was no parasitism in the birds that we killed. The adult-juvenile ratio, however, was about 50-50, which sounds a little like a cycle.

I thought you might be interested in the seminar schedule attached.

Bob is doing a good job writing up the Hungarian paper.

The invitation for a grouse hunt at the shack is hereby
extended, and I hope this war may be over before the next high.
Give my love to Betty.
Yours as ever,
Aldo

The agreeable arrangement Aldo referenced was Art's
flexible schedule he had with the Army which, according to
Betty, allowed time off for them to survey and band waterfowl
and shorebirds on nearby lakes and flooded fields. She noted,
"Art had a permit from the USFWS to trap and band ducks. In
nearby fields we put up our tents and set duck traps."
During those years in Texas, Aldo and Art kept in close
contact by mail. On April 7, 1943 the Professor wrote:

Dear Arthur:
You have certainly accumulated a surprising amount of good
data. I am sending the report to Albert.
I like all of your report except the management section. I
don't see any misfortune in having an undershot area. As for the
meat value of ducks, I can't go along at all. The gas, rubber, lead
and brass per pound would be shocking. I think the conference
went haywire trying to mix elk, deer, waterfowl, and small upland
game into one slogan.
Well, that's a small part of your very excellent report and
above is only my opinion.
Love to Elizabeth.
Yours as ever,
Aldo
Aldo Leopold

Later that month, on April 15th, 1943, he sent a copy of a letter written to a Mr. Albert F. Gallistel at the University Service Building:

Dear Albert:

My student Arthur Hawkins has checked up on Otto Lang's work as custodian on the Faville Prairie Natural Area and found that Lang has done all the work that was possible, considering the failure of the University to furnish him with materials for the gate, signs, fence maintenance, etc, or to authorize him to buy them. He is walked over the area at least once a month for a year; he has maintained the fence as far as could be done without materials; he is watched all neighboring cattle herds to see that none broke in, and he has checked all entering cars to ensure that they had a legitimate errand.

Hawkins thinks Lang would be willing to continue as custodian, despite the fact that he feels hurt that the verbal plans agree to by me a year ago have been carried out only from his side.

As I understand it, there are two paychecks due, for July 1947 and December 1947, at $25.00 each. I hope these can now be paid.

I understand that the last Arboretum Committee meeting turned over the custodial supervision to the Arboretum Biologist. Since he happens to be on my staff, I would now like written confirmation that the job is his, and that a specified fund is available for the maintenance of this area.

I asked permission, at the next meeting, to bring up some of the implications of this care as it affects our agreement with the Conservation Department.

Yours sincerely,
Aldo Leopold

On July 19th, 1943, Aldo wrote Art with some good news:

Dear Art:

The University Committee is outlining a general conservation course for undergraduates, and it seems likely that your Wildlife History of Faville Grove will be one of the readings. I have only 13 copies left. Do you have a supply at Faville Grove? If so, may I get an additional 15 copies? Would Mrs. Tillotson know where they are?

With best regards,
Aldo
Aldo Leopold

Later that same month, on July 30th, 1943, Aldo wrote Art, now a Sergeant at the Veterinary Service Station Hospital at Amarillo Army Air Field in Texas, the following letter full of news from home:

Dear Art:

I am asking Bob next time he goes out to bring back some reprints of the Fayville Grove history, and also Betty's prairie maps. Thanks for adding the 1941 map which will be carefully preserved.

I am glad you saw Bill Hamilton.

Jim Ayars' wood duck article came out in the July 31 issue of the Saturday Evening Post. If by any chance you do not get a copy, drop me a note and Alice will lay one aside for you. It's a pretty good job of popular interpretation.

Ted Frison was up yesterday, and I am glad to see that he wants to keep the waterfowl projects going, but finding personnel is, of course, difficult.

The Burlington folks were awfully glad to have you and Elizabeth stop off, and I am especially glad that you didn't miss Fritz entirely.

Starker is signing off from Missouri, and will be home for a month writing his thesis. (Maybe two months.) We expect him in a week or two.

All the wood ducks either failed to hatch or died except two which are thriving. Halpin says the air bubbles got burst in shipping, even in the fresh eggs. Maybe this is a hint for future shipments. Bob is raising a bunch of young Huns to get a final check on molts and bursa.

With best regards,
Yours as ever,
Aldo

Aldo's reference to the Burlington, Iowa visit referred to one of several times Art and Betty made while in route to Faville Grove near Lake Mills, Wisconsin. Art was on furlough from Texas. From Art's files:

"Betty and I stopped over at Burlington, Iowa, to visit the Leopolds, on our way home to Betty's home at Faville Grove, near Lake Mills, Wisconsin, 20 miles or so east of Madison. Betty had been working at the Post Exchanges.

While at the Leopold's we had the top floor bedroom of the old home which was occupied by Mrs. Leopold and her daughter Marie Leopold Lord. Two other houses on the bluff above the river where occupied by the Frederick Leopolds and the Carl Leopolds. We went with them that evening across the river to the Crystal Lake Club for a picnic where we sat on the ground around the fire, Mrs. Leopold in a low wicker chair.

During the War, cigarettes were hard to come by, but military personnel had access to them at the post exchanges, and we had brought cigarettes, though we ourselves did not smoke."

Art had two letters in his files from Aldo Leopold's mother, Clara Starker Leopold, who signed herself 'Mumsie". Here's one from 1945.

Dear Arthur and Betty;

Gift cigarettes I insist have an additional flavor and coming as such a complete surprise made them doubly enjoyed. I'm still an addict and claim they act both as a sedative and tonic. With Aldo and a Stella and Stella Jr spending the entire holiday week with me, the first time in thirty years, you can imagine how festive and gay the old home was. All told there were six in the three houses, all of them smokers, to make quick inroads on your generous donation. We are fairly steeped in our concern over the war. You will know about young Carl being in the Pacific, Aldo thinks now in Samoa, recently moved from his safe location. Bobby Lord a Captain in the Air Service in Italy and Luna was at Chenault (Chanute) Field (your ex home) last week, lecturing. Aldo dashed to Chicago for a glimpse of him, isn't he a bright chap?

Edith Jr seems to be enjoying a continuous fiesta. I'm glad you could take Betty home, it sounds very exciting to the homebody I've become with the scarcity of gas and the years piling up.

Betty reminds us so much of Starker's Betty and that is superlative praise – they look and act alike. Some day I may write you more fully – at present there are still a lot of thank you notes staring me in the face. Love to both and renewed thanks.

Mumsie

Art's and Betty's son Tex (Arthur Jr.) was born at Amarillo in December 1944, and they had sent the Leopolds an announcement. Clara "Mumsie" noted that in one of her 1945 letters:

"All news about young Arthur is gobbled up eagerly by the clan here. The announcement card is unique and lovely. I got mine, as did F & E.

Betty I share your mother's love for wide open spaces and the thrilling song of skylarks. The latter is in the past for me but I still pine for it.

Thanks a lot for your never failing thoughtfulness and be sure to stop over on your next trip home.

Always cordially,
Mumsie

Art also had letters in his files from two others of the Leopold clan. Starker, from Mexico on January 22, 1946 and Fred from Burlington on December 28, 1946. Both talked of hunting and game numbers. Both send their best to Betty and little Tex. From Starker in part:

"It was good to hear from you boy, and especially to know that you are out of uniform and back chasing geese. That must have been a hell of a slaughter at Horseshoe this fall– damn good thing that they had a set quota for the kill. Wish I could have tagged along with you getting weights and sexes.

Well this is sure a fine assignment I have as far as seeing new country goes. I know I've covered every state south and east of a line Nuvo Leon - Michoacan, and next week I am heading northwest to start working the Sierra Madre Occidental."

And from Fred in part:

"Edith had told me that she and her roommate, Mary, had discovered your January sixth scheduled talk on the Mississippi Valley Flyway Observations. The two of them will be on hand... Regarding observations on the flight in general, I would say that the flight this year was the smallest I can remember. As compared to the last two years, they were certainly less than half as many this year as in the two previous years.

I am in hopes that Dick Burrus will be able to send you his figures on the kill at Crystal Lake this year as compared to other years. He also may be able to give you some information on the sex ratios of the kill this year. I believe this will be reliable as far as Mallards are concerned but not on other species."

On December 31, 1947 Aldo Leopold gave the Introduction presentation at an Ecological Society conference in Chicago. he introduced a round table discussion on game and fur population mechanisms. Art had a copy of his five page introduction, which included:

"To illustrate three facts, more or less new, in population research. It is confined to game birds and game and fur mammals, not out of lack of interest in other groups, but because time does not suffice to cover a wider bracket"...

"One must conclude that we really know very little about population behavior, and that we are unable to manage wild animals until we know much more than we do now. Conservation then, as well as ecological science, demands a renewed effort to solve the problem of population mechanisms. This effort must dig deeper, must use more potent tools, and must expect to progress

more slowly and patiently than any made in the past."

That was presented on December 31, 1947. Leopold died less than four months later on April 21, 1948.

11

USFWS FLYWAY BIOLOGIST
DELTA MANITOBA (1946)

"Southward in fall and northward in spring, waterfowl have followed their ancestral travel routes or 'flyways' since the retreating glaciers left landmarks and watery stepping stones as guideposts."
– Art Hawkins, from the 1984 book, *Flyways – Pioneering Waterfowl Management in North America*

On January 23, 2015 the US Fish and Wildlife Service (USFWS) History named Art their Conservation Hero of the Week. The following is a tribute to his contributions while serving the Service.

"Art Hawkins was a waterfowl management pioneer in North America. Born in Batavia, New York, Hawkins enjoyed many outdoor pursuits as a boy, leading him to a career in conservation. Hawkins studied under Aldo Leopold and began his career with the U.S. Fish and Wildlife Service (USFWS) in 1946. He spent many summers with his wife, Betty, and young family living on the Canadian prairies

in a cabin with no running water, studying waterfowl and developing survey methods that are still in use today. Before recording equipment was available, Hawkins conducted aerial surveys with a notepad strapped to his leg, recording what he observed. Hawkins worked throughout the Mississippi Flyway and contributed greatly to the understanding of waterfowl ecology.

"It was through his dedication, leadership, and application of science that Hawkins demonstrated his greatest contribution to waterfowl conservation by making coordinated flyway management a reality. Hawkins was instrumental in the development and formation of the Flyway Councils. He served as the first USFWS representative for the Mississippi Flyway Council and recognized the need for individual flyway and species management plans, which he helped draft. In addition, he understood the need to include and account for the human dimension in waterfowl management. Hawkins retired from the Service in 1974. He was also a founding member of the Wood Duck Society and edited the text Flyways. He is remembered as a strong promoter of sportsmanship behavior and as a true gentleman dedicated to wildlife conservation."

John "Frosty" Anderson and Art Hawkins, trapping and banding ducks at the Chautauqua National Wildlife Refuge near Havana, IL, Nov. 1939. Studies continue until 1952 with more than 75,000 ducks banded.

Art Hawkins extracting his truck from a sand trap near the Forbes Lab.

The *Anax*, named after a genus of dragonfly, on the Illinois River at Havana on April 8, 1935. For a decade this 48-foot cabin boat served as the station's floating laboratory.

In 1939, Frank Bellrose and Art Hawkins lived on the Anax, docked at the Havana Coal docks on the Illinois River, until the lab was completed at the Forbes Biological Field Station, on the Chautauqua NWR. Bellrose, Hawkins, and Anderson occupy the new field station in 1940.

Art Hawkins watching waterfowl and hunters from a goose hunter's pit. Horseshoe Lake, February 1941.

Frank Bellrose examining a lead poisoning die-off at Rice Lake in March 1972.

John "Frosty" Anderson with lead-poisoned mallards, Lake Erie Marshes

John "Frosty" Anderson watching the waterfowl on the Mississippi, February 1941, shortly before joining the military along with Art Hawkins in May.

Fig. 4.—An X-ray head and fluoroscopic screen used at the Havana laboratory of the Illinois Natural History Survey to determine the incidence of ingested lead shot in wild waterfowl trapped alive as well as in dead and moribund birds picked up in the field. Each bird was placed in the cone, which was rotated in front of the fluoroscopic screen. This procedure presented to view more than one plane of the bird's body and thereby resulted in more precise location of pellets than was possible in a single plane view. (Photograph from the *Journal-Star*, Peoria, Illinois.)

X-ray and fluoroscopy were used to determine if lead shot had been ingested by ducks. Frank Bellrose (right) was the project leader.

Aldo Leopold provided office space for Art Hawkins after he joined the U.S. Fish and Wildlife Service in 1946, at the famous address: 424 University Farm Place, Madison, WI.

Delta Waterfowl and Wetland Research Station between Lake Manitoba and Codham Bay of Delta Marsh became the training ground for hundreds of waterfowl researchers.

Art was instrumental, along with Frank Bellrose, in erecting the first artificial wood duck nesting boxes.

The newly acquired airplane eliminated the problems of the muddy roads frequently encountered by the ground crews.

Lyle Sowls of the Delta staff pointing to a proposed stop on a trip we took in 1946 to many waterfowl areas north and west to the Peace River, Alberta.

Standing left-right: Jim Huston, Bob McCabe, Pete Ward, Lew Rowinski, Walter Breckridge, Walter Crissey, George Brakhage, Chuck Southwick Kneeling: Nick Neufeldt, Bill Elder, Lyle Sowls, Gene Bassenmaier, Keith Story, Art Hawkins (USFWS photo)

Duck survey team at Delta: Lyle Sowls, Albert Hachbaum, Bob Smith, Art Hawkins, Peter Ward, and Dave Spencer – jaunty young biologists.

Art Hawkins with the Sea-B, affectionately known as the "Flying Stove," landed on a northern lake (probably Granville Lake), 1951

Art Hawkins surveying for waterfowl on Lake Manitoba at Delta Waterfowl and Wetland Research Station probably – 1951 or earlier.

On March 9, 2000 in an interview with Mark Madison of the USFWS History, Art described in his own words his time employed with the USFWS.

"After that (Leopold's death) I moved to the Region 3 office in Minneapolis. Although my supervision as a flyway biologist was out of Washington, I was based in Region 3 because it was handy to a lot of good waterfowl activity. I was also spending much of my time in Canada. I actually spent about half the year in Canada during that period. I took my family with me, and we based at Delta Waterfowl Research Station. I worked out from there. We had a plane there, too. I shared time between aerial and ground transects.

"One of the things I remember most about that period was the wonderful cooperation we had from the Manitoba people. Jerry Malaher was the Game Branch Director at the time, and he was wonderfully cooperative. If it hadn't been for him, I wonder how the whole U.S.-Canadian relations would have ended up, after having gotten off to a shaky start. It was wonderful cooperation that we had.

"We took the family up there for eight years, usually arriving at Delta in April, about the time the ducks were just getting there. At this time, we were trying to develop a system for counting ducks on breeding grounds. With a lot of cooperation from Delta Waterfowl research personnel, we established some experimental transects where we compared what we saw on the ground with what the aerial crew counted. We even tried canoe transects, versus aerial transects to get some notion of relative visibility of different species on the ground versus in the air. Then we established a grid system of running transects which followed east-west lines with a width of one-eighth of a mile on either side of the path of the plane. Along these transects we counted all of the ducks that fell on either side of the transect line. This is the same system they use today.

"Before me, Bob Smith was the Mississippi Flyway Biologist for the Fish and Wildlife Service. He then took up flying. After the war was over, the Service acquired free airplanes from the military, including Stinson L-5's, which were observation planes during the war. Armed with this new way of counting ducks, Bob left for Canada in his plane, while I drove his car. We met at Delta, and started our work together, working closely with the Delta biologists. The following year, Dave Spencer joined us in Manitoba. Dave was probably the most advanced in statistics of any of us. He had taken a course in college, which the rest of us hadn't. He had a copy of Snedacor's book on statistics, and taught us a lot about sampling procedures. This was really the start of a statistical approach there, with the width of the transect one-eighth of a mile, every four miles you advanced you would sample one square mile. Little by little, we divided the breeding grounds into units based on density of potholes, and the density of the ducks. The sampling frequency differed, in these different units, depending on the relative abundance of water, and duck density. Little by little the whole system evolved. With a few modifications, it is pretty much the same today as it was then.

"Ground to air comparisons also started early on. In these, one crew would beat out the transects on the ground, and within 24 hours, the aerial crew would count over the same area. You then had a direct comparison with what they saw, with what the ground crew saw. From those figures, you could make adjustments to the duck population count. For example, mallard and canvasbacks were very visible compared to teal. You might have a correction factor of less than two for mallards or canvasbacks, but it could be as high as fifteen for green winged teal. You had to take visibility differences into consideration in order to come up with reasonably reliable figures. Ground-air comparisons are still being made every year. They automatically adjust for differences in observer abilities. You can't use a "constant" from year to year because the visibility changes depending on whether or not the aspen leaves have come out, and a whole lot of things like that. You have to make this correction on an annual basis.

"So, anyway at that early time, we were very much in the banding mode too. We were trying to establish techniques for catching young ducks. Heavy equipment gradually got better and easier to use, and finally became more efficient than 10 when we first started out. We put on some huge drives in some concentration areas where there would be thousands of mostly adult male molting ducks.

"We were also involved in things such as "die offs" due to things like botulism, and trying to do something about that. We picked up sick ducks, or drove the birds away or whatever seemed most appropriate. In early July, it was time to start surveys again to see how the production was, in relation to breeding pairs found in the spring. Late in the season, we were still trying to catch more ducks to get them banded to see what flight lanes they were taking out of Canada into the States, and also to see what flyways they affected most. We were kept very busy, right up to the beginning of the hunting season.

"During the hunting season, I usually went up to the Pas area of Manitoba, and started checking ducks and geese that were taken by hunters, to obtain information on species shot, and to get an idea of what the age ratio was. This was to see how many young ducks were being produced and shot.

"My family and I remained in Canada until the opening

of the hunting season in the States. Then I would return home leaving my family there, and would work as a flyway biologist through all the states of the Mississippi Flyway. I tried to time it so that I would hit each state at about the beginning of the hunting season. At that time, Patuxent was working on a method of collecting wings, and determining what the age ratio was from the wing samples. At first, we weren't able to age the birds. We went through a series of years, checking techniques to determine the age of the birds by their wing patterns. We finally became confident about obtaining actual figures on success rates by species for any given year."

12

FLYWAYS

In May of 1984, the United States Department of the Interior Fish and Wildlife Service published the book *Flyways Pioneering Waterfowl Management in North America.* Art was co-editor with Rossalius C. Hanson, Harvey K. Nelson, and H. M. Reeves. In the introduction of this 517 page classic historic book, the editors "regret that this volume could not be more complete. However, we believe that it accurately portrays the problems, the spirit of adventure and accomplishments of an era when waterfowl management in North America was in its early stages...Waterfowl management has come a long way in the past 60 years but still has some distance to go before the future of the waterfowl resource is secure."

Art's contributions to the book were bountiful. He touts Aldo Leopold's critical contributions to early waterfowl management. And he began in Chapter 1, *The U.S. Response*, which follows:

Southward in fall and northward in spring, waterfowl have followed their ancestral travel routes or "flyways" since the retreating glaciers left landmarks and watery stepping stones as guideposts. Observers noted these bird migrations for centuries, but here in North America, not until the present century were the routes delineated and given names.

Flyways became apparent largely as a result of a technique call banding. John James Audubon, the great American artist, was credited with using silver wires to legband a brood of phoebes in 1803. Two of his banded phoebes returned the following year, completing the first banding study. Dr. Leon J. Cole, professor at the University of Wisconsin, used leg bands to mark pigeons he was studying and, with P.A. Taverner of Canada, was instrumental in organizing the American Bird Banding Association in 1909. In 1920 their records and subsequent administration of the banding program was turned over to the U.S. Bureau of Biological Survey (USBS), with Frederic C. Lincoln in charge.

Even before the banding technique was developed, much was known about bird migration. In 1915, Wells W. Cooke, Biological Survey biologist, published a government bulletin on bird migration, noting that "the survey has been collecting data on bird migration for more than 25 years." This information came from "more than 2,000 different observers," including "field naturalists" and "lighthouse keepers." Cooke presented maps showing migration routes of several species but lacked banding data to support his conclusions, conclusions that were remarkably accurate considering his handicaps.

Frederick C. Lincoln – in 1935 and again in 1950 – updated Cooke's bulletin on migration, adding information strengthened by the new file on banded birds. A manual for bird banders issued in 1929 showed that more than 400,000 birds (all species) had been banded in Canada and the United States, producing 19,000 usable recovery records. The file had grown to "well over 2,500,000 entries" by 1935. A decade later "nearly 5,000,000 birds had been banded," producing "more than 300,000 usable return records." About twelve hundred ducks were banded on the Great Salt Lake marshes of Utah from 1914-1916 by Alexander Wetmore during his duck-sickness studies. Lincoln developed a waterlily-leaf trap that caught about two thousand ducks in Illinois River marshes during March 1922, the first large-scale banding of waterfowl.

According to Lincoln, "Recovery of banded ducks and geese accumulated so rapidly that by 1920 it was possible to map out the four waterfowl flyways' great geographical regions, each with breeding and wintering grounds connected by a complicated series of migration routes." Thus, the flyway concept was conceived at about the same time that the great drought of the 1930s spread over the land, parching the nesting grounds and leaving the waterfowl population in shambles.

Most of us have heard about the "dirty thirties" and how the waterfowl resource was blighted by the prolonged drought. Only a few are aware that duck numbers were also perceived as slumping before the turn of the century. We are inclined to envision the "good old days" as a time when the woods, prairies and marshes abounded with wildlife, and all the waters teemed with fish. That might have been true, relatively speaking, but some old-timers who were keen observers saw it differently. Dr. Clarence M. Weed and Dr. Ned Dearborn, both highly educated and well-qualified professionals, were two such observers. In 1903 they wrote a book containing much information about waterfowl and the people who enjoyed them. As they saw it: "The stock of wildfowl has reached a low ebb through a long-continued and ever-increasing persecution and an ever-narrowing breeding range. Two different motive forces have pushed the persecution – the market and an inborn love of hunting, the one commercial (a matter of dollars and cents) the other a natural instinct."

But in this dark hour the authors offered hope. "By care the stock may be replenished and the birds indefinitely preserved – a continued source of benefit to us and a worthy legacy to posterity."

Even in the first years of this century the roots of the problem were apparent. Migratory birds could not receive the protection they needed without more uniform harvest regulations. The Lacey Act, passed by the U.S. Congress in 1900, recognized this need. It prohibited interstate commerce of wildlife contrary to laws of the states involved. It prohibited the importation of foreign wildlife without a federal permit, and it gave the USDA new responsibilities concerning the preservation, distribution, introduction, and restoration of wildlife.

Weed and Dearborn gave examples of the dissimilar state hunting regulations. For example, ducks could not be taken in Iowa from April 15 to September 1, while in adjacent Minnesota the closed dates were January 1 to September 1, and in Missouri (also adjacent to Iowa), April 1 to October 1. From these and other similar cases the authors concluded, "This condition of things is manifestly wrong, and so long as it continues the laws in question are certain to be violated." Realistically, they pointed out, "If game laws do not meet the approval and have the hearty support of the masses, they are void."

Reacting to this lack of uniformity in game laws, Charles Hallock, as early as 1897, suggested to the National Game, Bird and Fish Protective Association that the United States be divided into three districts – Northern, Southern, and Pacific – within which similar game laws would be adopted. (Except for Arizona, which was placed in the Southern District, Hallock's Pacific District was identical to the Pacific Flyway as delineated a half-century later.) But Hallock was ahead of his time. States still were unwilling to relinquish their jurisdiction over the taking of wildlife.

George Shiras III, then U.S. Congressman from Pennsylvania but better known as an outstanding nature photographer, was among those convinced that the trend in waterfowl numbers would continue downward until migratory birds were placed under centralized federal control. The bill he introduced in 1904 supported this conviction but, like Hallock's idea, had little chance for passage.

After nearly a decade of intensive lobbying and salesmanship by conservation leaders, the Migratory Bird Act was signed into law by President Taft on March 4, 1913. It empowered the secretary of agriculture to set the dates for hunting migratory game birds, "having due regard to the zones of temperature, and to the distribution, abundance, economic value, breeding habits and times and lives of migratory flight of such birds." Among those most responsible for the Act's passage were John B. Burnham of the American Game Protective Association (founded in 1911); Dr. T. Gilbert Pearson, secretary of the National Association of Audubon Societies (founded in 1901); and Charles Sheldon of the Boone and Crockett Club. The Weeks-McLean Bill, which upon passage became the act, was guided through the House by Representative Weeks of Massachusetts and through the Senate by Senator McLean of Connecticut. It was patterned after the Shiras Bill but was broadened to include non-game migratory birds, as well as those classes as game.

These conservation-minded legislators had to overcome strong opposition to their bill not only from unrelenting state-righters but also from market hunters whose income was threatened and sportsmen who enjoyed spring shooting. On a broader front, the act immediately came under fire from those who questioned its constitutionality. In 1914, a U.S. District Court judge at Jonesboro, Arkansas, at the trial of the *United States v. Harvey C. Shauver*, found the act unconstitutional.

Meanwhile, to counter the question of constitutionality (at the suggestion of Justice Elihui Root), a small group commenced drafting a treaty between the United States and Canada for the protection of migratory birds. A draft prepared by W.S. Haskell, legal council for the American Game Protective Association , was rejected. Then, Dr. T. S. Palmer of the Biological Survey wrote the draft that three years later in 1916, with few changes, was ratified by Great Britain for Canada and by the United States. In Canada, Dr. C. Gordon Hewitt, Dominion consulting zoologist did most of the legwork that finally resulted in the treaty's acceptance. Other Canadians who deserve special credit for its passage were Honorable Martin Burrell, minister of agriculture, Clifford Sifton, chairman of the Commission of Conservation; J. B. Harkins of Canadian National Parks; James White, deputy head of the Conservation Commission; and several officers of Canadian Railroads who took special interest in this project. In the United States, Dr. E. W. Nelson became chief of the Biological Survey in 1916, and it was his job to implement the provisions of the legislation.

Ratification of the Migratory Bird Treaty removed the need for a Supreme Court ruling on the constitutionality of the Migratory Bird Act, but one important step remained passage of an enabling act. This act passed on June 6, 1918, giving the USBS responsibility for its enforcement. Opponents, however, still didn't accept defeat. In 1920 following a test case, *Missouri v. Holland* (the U.S. government's enforcement officer), the Supreme Court ruled in favor of Holland in a landmark decision read by Justice Oliver Wendell Holmes. This decision cleared the way for a new era in the appreciation, use, and management of the continent's migratory birds.

Early in the 1930s when hunting seasons were being restricted, a foundation called More Game Birds in America (the forerunner to Ducks Unlimited) complained that "in the past three years, the open seasons for migratory waterfowl have been changed five times, culminating in the highly unsatisfactory 30-day season for 1931…. Last year, in the neighboring states of Missouri, Illinois, Indiana, and Kentucky, there were four different seasons for waterfowl shooting fixed by Federal regulations."

Hallock's idea of thirty-five years earlier was resurrected and embellished with a series of maps showing temperature zones across the country on the first day of each month from October through January and the average date when the mean temperature dropped below 32 degrees Fahrenheit. These weather maps were then converted into three north-south "waterfowl season zones." Apparently in response to the foundation's suggestion, the three hunting season zones set by the secretary during the late 1930s corresponded closely to those of More Game Birds. After that they became increasingly complicated by exceptions and modifications, until the north-south format was dropped and an east-west flyway system was adopted in 1948.

Excellence scientific studies and biological literature on waterfowl and other migratory birds existed long before the Migratory Bird Treaty Act was ratified. However, the emphasis was changed by the treaty and its obligations, at least as far as the federal government was concerned. The American Ornithological Union deserves much credit for the establishment in 1884 of an office of Economic Ornithology in the USDA to study and publish the food habits and migration of birds and other wildlife.

In 1905 this office became the USBS. Their publications dealt primarily with food and other habits of birds, their economic status (especially in relation to agriculture), and the new laws for their protection.

By 1918 the staff of young Biological Survey had published at least two dozen free or inexpensive pamphlets on migratory birds. These pamphlets featured the results of several food habit studies and instructions for raising ducks or attracting birds with birdhouses and food. Information about the migration and distribution of birds, and game laws also was available.

In the early years, the food habits laboratory was the busiest place in the Survey. Here most of the new generation of waterfowl biologists received their indoctrination. Soon the declining status of waterfowl and their habitats would require major attention, but not yet. This was the lull before the storm.

In a report recounting the progress made during the first decade under the Migratory Bird Treaty Act, and Audubon Society spokesman stated, "The number of wildfowl have so increased since 1913 as to astonish the country." Surprisingly enough, in this report from an organization often considered lukewarm toward hunting is the following statement: "Ducks exist in enormous numbers throughout the continent... We must think of them in terms of tens of millions and not feel alarmed that several million are killed each year. They are very prolific."

But this mood of complacency was soon shattered by Director Nelson of the Biological Survey. In the mid-1920s he wrote: "The danger to the perpetualism of the stock of wildfowl is so great and so imminent... that there is the most vital need for all conservationists and lovers of wildlife to sink petty differences of opinion as to the details and to unite in constructive work to insure the future of our migratory game birds."

Warnings such as those of Dr. Nelson had to be based on more than food habits studies on instructions on how to raise ducks. And they were. Fieldmen under his direction were beginning to look at waterfowl status and their overall well-being, as they were obliged to do by the Migratory Bird Treaty. The Audubon report of 1926 gave the Survey a high score in meeting this responsibility. "Congress has given complete administrative power to the Department of Agriculture, acting through the Biological Survey... It has fulfilled its responsibilities and produced satisfactory results." The report pointed out that "the supply can only be approximately determined by a detailed study of continental conditions by trained men... The Department has in the Biological Survey the only organization competent to solve these problems." This was a fine tribute to the fieldmen who soon would be known as "flyway biologists."

During the 1920s a start was made by Congress toward creating a national refuge system, with separate acts establishing the Upper Mississippi River Wildlife and Fish Refuge in 1924, and the Bear River Migratory Bird Refuge in 1929. The Migratory Bird Conservation Act, passed in 1929, authorized the appropriation of $7.9 million for the purchase or lease of refuges for waterfowl, and in the western provinces of Canada more than a dozen lakes and marshes were designated as inviolate sanctuaries.

Another major development in 1929 was the presentation by Chairman Aldo Leopold of his committee's report on an American Wildlife policy stated that "the management measures most needed are the public acquisition of habitats threatened with drainage, the establishment of a continental system of public and private refuges, and a more adequate program of fact finding." The report added, "There is pressing need to know more about the status, not only of migratory game crop as a whole, but of each constituent species." Singling out defects in the current program, the report states that "its stock of facts is inadequate. Research must keep ahead, not lag behind the need for facts. Game yields can be greatly increased, and the costs and risks of management decreased, by more research."

This recognition of the need for research to make possible an improved program, coming as it did from the leading conservationists of that day, couldn't have occurred at a better time. A drought was setting in on the western plains of North America that was to become the most severe in history. Concurrently, a major economic depression nearly paralysed the nation.

Sometimes a near-catastrophe is a blessing in disguise. Such was the case, so far as waterfowl were concerned in the 1930s when dust blotted out the midday sun throughout the midlands of North America. Marshlands, parched from years of deficient rainfall, became mudflats that caked and crumbled and added to the rolling clouds as the dust bowl expanded. Even the casual observer knew that all wildlife that depend on wetlands was in serious trouble.

According to a USDA report published in 1934, "Serious drought conditions have arisen periodically throughout recorded history, always doubtless working hardships on waterfowl. But never, so far as is known, have there been so many destructive conditions and agencies at work at once upon a depleted waterfowl supply as during the past 5 years... The support and interest of all public-spirited citizens are now needed to repair the damage."

Threat drought of the thirties was devastating because of its duration. According to Bell and Preble, writing in 1934:

The long period of deficient precipitation over hundreds of thousands of square miles of the finest breeding territory in the North Central States and the southern parts of the Prairie Provinces of Canada began in 1915. With the exception of a slightly increased rainfall in 1920, this shortage continued til 1924, when all available records for duration of time, extent of territory affected, and severity of drought conditions were broken. Serious drought conditions have arisen periodically throughout recorded history, always doubtless working hardships upon the waterfowl. But never, so far as is known, have there been so many destructive conditions and agencies at work at once upon a depleted waterfowl supply as during the past five years. During that period the number of waterfowl have fall drastically. The support and interest of all public-spirited citizens are now needed to repair the damage...

So alarming was the situation facing waterfowl that J. Clark Salyer, also in 1934, wrote, "This nesting grounds now lies as a desert so far as its millions of waterfowl are concerned. The sturdy human stock of the prairie lands will endure. The herds will grow fat again. But can the earlier inhabitants, the winged millions, reestablish themselves in all their early abundance?"

But the dust clouds had a silver lining. Thanks to the leadership of people like Aldo Leopold and J.N. "Ding" Darling in the United States, and Hoyes Lloyd in Canada, the North American public responded as it usually does when the chips are down. A blueprint for action was ready in the form of the American Game Policy and, despite a depression, the money was available from President Franklin D. Roosevelt's emergency programs. Private interests rose to the occasion under the banners of the National

Wildlife Federation, the Wildlife Management Institute, and Ducks Unlimited.

The 1930s were trying years in more ways than one for those responsible for managing the waterfowl resource. As conditions got tougher, tempers flared. Hunting regulations became progressively more restrictive, much to the dismay of hunters. But to the non-hunters and many conservationists, all hunting should have been banned for the duration of the emergency. The Biological Survey, which was responsible for the regulations, thus caught criticism from both sides of the issue.

Representing United States sportsmen, the More Game Birds in America Foundation reported on a survey they sponsored, and two years later the same organization conducted and reported on the *1935 International Wild Duck Census*. Their findings agreed with those of Biological Survey investigators, but the two organizations drew different conclusions. Whereas the Survey pointed to the shotgun as a major cause of the decline and saw tighter harvest regulations as a means of helping the situation, More Game Birds stated that "this is no time to experiment with substitutes or to squabble about petty, unpopular and unenforceable shooting restrictions presumed to provide the remedy." The Survey's position was weakened in the eyes of strict conservationists by permitting the continuance of two deadly hunting techniques, baiting and using live decoys. Nor did a faux pas committee by the USBS in 1934 escape the attention of the critics. A critic named Irving Brant pointed out that "the so-called 'staggered season' which the United States Bureau of Biological Survey established in 1934, actually wrote into the law the precise method of 'rest days' by which the heaviest slaughter of ducks is obtained on baited shooting grounds." Subsequent analysis of banding data showed that this criticism was justified, and the mistake was not repeated.

Lest the Biological Survey receive all the blame for questionable decisions on hunting regulations made during those crucial years it should be pointed out that then, as now, decisions were influenced by recommendations of an advisory board. It has been claimed that this twenty-member board, during those years, was dominated by Eastern duck club members, a fact that explains the majority votes against shortening the season, lowering the bag limit, and abolishing baiting.

A major problem of that era was enforcement. Market hunting still flourished in parts of the country and general unrest among hunters led to a level of violations far beyond the capability of the two dozen federal law officers to combat. To make matters worse, new automotive transportation was rapidly increasing the mobility of hunters. Meanwhile developers and farmers were taking advantage of the drought to drain wetlands previously too difficult to reach.

A shortage of funds had severely limited the activities of the young Biological Survey, but this situation changed rapidly for the better during the 1930s. The seed of an idea germinating for several years finally sprouted in the form of companion bills introduced by Congressman Richard Kleberg from Texas and Senator Frederic C. Walcott from Connecticut. These bills became the Migratory Bird Hunting Stamp Act of 1934. Roosevelt, who had just become President, had commenced concocting his "alphabet soup' series of programs aimed at putting depressed America back to work through public works programs. Suddenly millions of dollars became available for the acquisition and development of waterfowl habitat.

But the money did not come easily. It took a super salesman named Ding Darling, during the few months he served as Survey chief, to implement the program designed by a special committee appointed by President Roosevelt. Darling, Aldo Leopold, and Thomas Beck prepared this blueprint. Considerably fewer funds would have gone into wildlife projects without such a plan, which emphasized the need for waterfowl habitat and fact finding. Ding Darling was the Billy Sunday and Billy Graham of the conservation movement, all wrapped into one. Probably no conservation leader before or since has so effectively united the various conservation interests of the nation in a common cause.

As chief of the Biological Survey, Darling needed a strong personality to carry out his ambitious program – and in J. Clark Salyer he found the ideal man. Salyer was put in charge of the newly created Division of Migratory Waterfowl. With $8.5 million in emergency funds at his disposal, Salyer began the task of building a migratory birds refuge system, became the world's largest.

Another positive and epochal development during the early 1930s was the publication of Aldo Leopold's classic book, *Game Management*. It heralded a new era in the outlook toward wildlife and the way it was managed. Two concepts Leopold introduced in that work were unknown outside the professional management community for four decades, but today "ecology" and "the environment" are everyday words. In 1933 Leopold described the same phenomenon for the word "conservation". He wrote:

"Came then Theodore Roosevelt with the idea of 'conservation through wise use'. Wildlife, forests, ranges, and waterpower were conceived by him to be *renewable organic resources*, which might last forever if they were *harvested scientifically, and not faster than they reproduced.*

Conservation had until then been a lowly word, sleeping obscurely in the back of the dictionary. The public had never hear it. It carried no particular connotation of woods or waters. Overnight it became the label of a national issue."

Leopold reinterpreted and added scope to the Roosevelt conservation doctrine. Leopold conceived of natural resources as one integral whole, conservation as a public responsibility, and wildlife management as the means for discharging that responsibility. In *Game Management* for the first time conservation leaders and students had a reference for exploring the principles and approaches that would make "conservation" and wildlife management interdependent. Above all, Leopold emphasized the role of science and the need for research.

The stage was now set for wildlife management to become a recognized profession and for the flyway system of managing waterfowl to become a recognized profession and for the flyway system of managing waterfowl to become recognized as one of its towering accomplishments. Management has come a long way since Audubon first banded those phoebes, eighteen decades ago!

13

ALDO LEOPOLD AND PIONEERING GAME MANAGEMENT

On the 24th of August in 2003, I attended the Leopold Education Project (LEP) National Workshop where Art Hawkins presented a talk entitled "Pioneering in Waterfowl Management". Art was 89 years old at the time, but still sharp as a tack. He kept the audience spellbound as he celebrated the seventieth anniversary of the publication of Aldo Leopold's distinguished book, *Game Management* - and shared his album of memories as a game manager with the Illinois Natural History Survey waterfowl studies. In the audience was Nina Leopold Bradley, Aldo's daughter and close friend of Art. Pay close attention to Art's look at Leopold's discussion on the importance of people management as part of wildlife management.

He began,

"Included with the LEP announcement to you about this workshop was the copy of a paper by Clay Schoenfeld entitled "Fifty Years of Aldo Leopold's Game Management". Starting with this statement: "The year 1983 will mark the fiftieth anniversary of the publication of Aldo Leopold's monumental book, Game Management." I hope you all read it. Today we celebrate the 70th anniversary of this book, which to me is still the foremost book on this subject ever written.

My favorite review of this book was by Dr. Raymond F. Dasmann, Professor of Ecology at U. of California Santa Cruz in the book, *Aldo Leopold-the man and his legacy/ 1987* I quote: "During my undergraduate education,... I was introduced to what had become the standard textbook in wildlife courses, Aldo Leopold's *Game Management*. It was more than a textbook; it was a beautifully written volume that skilfully presented the knowledge of wildlife management up to that time. More than any other single contribution, it established the field of wildlife management as both a science and an art. Then, during my first year as a graduate student *A Sand County Almanac* was published...both books made powerful impression on my own thinking...when I again read *Game Management* recently, I was impressed with its current relevance. It was not outdated...most of Leopold's basic concept remains sound and useful...In many ways America was a much nicer place to live when Leopold wrote *Game Management* ....there were only half as many Americans and wildlands were far more extensive than today. Americans as people tended to be more secure and more confident despite the economic disruption caused by the Depression and the Dust Bowl (of the 1930s)."

I agree with Dasmann that the book, *Game Management* contains more, a lot more, than a textbook usually offers. Not to be critical of my former professor, but I suspect that the readership of this classic would have been increased many-fold over the years had the title been other than *Game Management.* The word game probably turned away thousands of non-hunters. "Wildlife", rather than game in the title would have been better but even that short-changes the overall scope of this book which includes much on people management as well as wildlife. Part III, in fact, is entirely on the people factor, perhaps most important limiting factor of all. Why is this book important reading for all of us here today, whether or not you approve of hunting as a sport? Read the first sentence of the first chapter of G.M. which says: "Game management is the art of making land produce sustained annual crops of wild game for recreational use." Substitute the word wildlife for "game" and does anyone have a problem with that? Or, do you have any problems with the stated objective of the book: "to portray the mechanism which produces all species on all lands rather than to prescribe the procedures for producing particular species or managing particular lands".

Is G. M. just about producing game? Here are some quotes answering that question:

"The objective of a conservation program for non-game wildlife should be exactly parallel today (to that of game management): to retain for the average citizen the opportunity to see, admire and enjoy, and the challenge to understand, the varied forms of birds and mammals indigenous to (your) state. It implies not only that these forms are kept in existence but that the greatest possible variety of them exist in each community."

Leopold makes no bones about it: these good things won't happen unless (and I quote) "we can see the issue as a mutual problem (confronting everyone) salable (only) by their mutual cooperation." He goes on: "There is in short fundamental unity of purpose and method between bird-lovers and sportsman. This common task of teaching the public how to modify economic activities for conservation purposes...The hope of the future lies not in curbing the influence of human occupancy—it's already too late for that—but in creating a better understanding of the extent of that influence and a new ethic governance." Leopold had no patience with quibbling over details or petty arguments. Either we have a land ethic or we don't and it's up to education, like those assembled here, to put the ideas across. G.M. was the textbook for Leopold's class numbered 118. I passed the course 67 years ago and my slides show where it led me.

*****

The month following his presentation in Baraboo Art wrote,

Dear Ken:
Guess our letters crossed in the mail. Thanks for the kind words. Thanks for enclosing the article waterfowl forecast by Nickens. I wonder if Nickens was a hunter (he still spells widgeon with a d) and seems quite gullible about accepting numbers without any reservations "the word from DUCKVILLE this year GET READY". Of course he is not alone. Duck stamp sales should be up. As you know a lot of ducks failed in their first nesting attempt and try again and again. After unexpectedly good water this spring, the drought returned in many areas. Many shallow wetlands dried up and I wonder how that may have affected the late hatch. We'll have to wait and see how it all played out.
I haven't seen Ed since you took the pic of us with your dog. We're scheduled to get together this week so I hope he brings it along. Today is duck season opener and the weather looks perfect for it. I'll leave as soon as I write this to make the rounds and see how many hunters are out. I checked a duck pass twice this week (as I have over the last 20 or so years) and night before last the ringnecks were No. 1. I counted 300 in one hr. around

sunset. *Mallards, woodies and blue wing had declined since an earlier count. They may have been sitting tight in the rice bed of one of the lakes.*

If you get over this way be sure to stop by.
Best wishes for the hunting season,
Art Hawkins

14

ALDO LEOPOLD, ORNITHOLOGIST THE IVORY-BILLED WOODPECKER AND ME (2005)

A rt presented the following talk at the Leopold Education Project (LEP) 10th Annual National Workshop in Baraboo, Wisconsin on August 21, 2005.

"In November 1934 I was a grad student in fisheries at Cornell University in Ithaca, New York. Two months later, on January 2, 1935 to be exact, I had lunch with Nina and Estella Leopold and their parents at their home in Madison, Wisconsin. That morning I had become Professor Aldo Leopold's third student. I could thank my lucky stars that this happened but instead I owe it to ornithology, the study of birds. More specifically I owe it to 3 particular birds, the ruffed grouse, the bobwhite quail and most of all to the Ivory-billed woodpecker. That, I realize, requires some explanation. But first you need to understand something about the time period in which this happened.

It was in the depth of America's worst depression. The western plains were in the throes of the worst drought in history called the "dirty thirties". Wetlands were dry and ducks at the lowest point ever. Bread lines were long and any job was something to cherish. Eighteen months before I arrived, Aldo Leopold had become the first professor of game management in the country at a salary of $8,000 to cover all expenses of his department. His classic book "Game Management" had just been published but only after he had agreed to contribute $500 to offset some publication costs. As his research assistant working toward my degree I was to receive a monthly stipend of $60. Ten days after I arrived, perhaps to celebrate his 49th birthday, he and his friend Ed Ochner took a trip through the countryside in search of a base for hunting. That's when they found the Shack which would become the Mecca for conservationists around the world and soon to be part of the National Aldo Leopold Legacy Center.

Aldo Leopold wore many hats - forester, teacher, writer, father of this and that, and many other hats. Luckily for me one of his hats bore the label "ornithologist". My new professor and I had one thing in common, our attachment to birds, but how did this one thing bring us together?

Here's how: The professor was a hunter and his favorite game bird was the ruffed grouse. My dossier, when I applied for my job, showed that I had worked part time in the New York State grouse survey, one of the earliest and largest investigations of game bird populations in the country. I suspect that he chose me largely because of that experience. Thus the grouse ranks among my three top birds including the fact that it also was my favorite bird to hunt. I was hired to study the bobwhite quail which I knew little about but I think my grouse experience made up for this lack, in the Professor's evaluation of my limited credentials. Thus the bob white joins the grouse on my hit list. But what about the Ivory-bill my third special bird and perhaps the most important of the three in determining my future? That's a longer story and one I'll tell here in some depth because it's so timely. Back at Cornell on that fateful November day for me, my advisor Dr. Arthur Allen called me into his office. Another grad student, Jim Tanner, already was there. Doc told us that he had just learned of two job opportunities and wondered if we might be interested, already knowing that we both were short of funds. One opening was to study the endangered Ivory-bill; the other the bobwhite quail in Wisconsin. Jim was doing his grad work in ornithology while I was in fisheries so he had first choice and, without hesitation chose the Ivory-bill study. I immediately applied for the bobwhite job, was accepted, and during Christmas vacation packed all my belongings in my Model A Ford coupe and headed for Wisconsin. That's how I was able to have lunch with the Leopolds on January 2, 1935, at their home.

In the spring of 1936 Dr. Allen, my advisor at Cornell, came to Wisconsin while on a lecture tour for the National Audubon Society. He was introduced by Professor Leopold. In 1935, Dr. Allen had led an expedition to the Singer Tract in Louisiana and there, in company with Jim Tanner, Professor Peter Paul Kellogg and artist Dr. George Miksch Sutton had filmed and obtained sound of the Ivory-bill, the last recorded until 2004. The Ivory bill findings were a major part of his lecture in Madison. Afterwards, my two major professors Allen and Leopold and I had a brief discussion about old times. Dr. Allen told us that he wished he could see and hear prairie chickens. By then I was manager of the Faville Grove Wildlife Experimental Area. We told Dr. Allen that if he could be at Faville Grove by sun-up next day we'd fulfill his wish. This we did and, as a bonus as we were leaving the booming ground area after watching the chickens perform, we stumbled on a prairie chicken nest which gave Dr. Allen an extra thrill. As it turned out, the Faville Grove prairie was soon ditched to become a cow pasture and the chickens vanished. The nest we found and Dr. Allen filmed was the last prairie chicken nest ever found on Faville Prairie.

Dr. Allen, Professor Leopold and the Ivory-bill thus have strong connectivity in my recollections. Evidently influenced by the findings of this Allen Expedition in 1935 and by a book by Dr. Hornaday on "Our Vanishing Wildlife species", Leopold wrote an essay published in 1936 called "Threatened Species." I quote from that essay: "Certain ornithologists have discovered a remnant of the Ivory-billed woodpecker, a bird inextricably interwoven with our pioneer tradition... It is known that the Ivory-bill requires as its habitat large stretches of virgin hardwoods. The present remnant lives in such a forest owned and held by an industry as reserve stumpage. Cutting may begin and the Ivory-bill may be done for at any moment. The Park service has or can get funds to buy virgin forests, but it does not know the Ivory-bill or its predicament. It is absorbed in the intricate problem of accommodating the public which is mobbing its parks. When it buys a new park it is likely to do so in some scenic spot with the general objective of making room for visitors rather than the specific objective of perpetuating some specific thing. Is it not time to establish particular parks or their equivalent for particular natural wonders like the Ivory-bill?" As I continue my story, note the parallel between this Leopold essay and the present situation regarding the Ivory-bill discovery.

Seventy years have passed since the Allen Expedition to the Singer Tract and Leopold's statement on the Ivory-bill was written, but earlier this year this spectacular bird again makes headlines in papers across the country. For many years written-off as extinct by all but a few hard-core birders, an Ivory-bill is discovered-alive! It was found in the heavily wooded bottomlands and hardwood terraces of the Cache River and Bayou DeView in Arkansas, a habitat similar in many ways to the Singer Tract in Louisiana. The Singer Tract, where the last nesting area of the Ivory-bill was found, was reduced to cropland by money-hungry timber barons. The Cache bottomlands almost suffered a similar fate thirty years ago, this time at the hands of the U.S. Government. Thanks to the intervention of conservationists like Dr. Rex Hancock and the Arkansas Wildlife Federation the plan to channelize the Cache and convert 170 thousand acres to cropland was blocked. A major wintering area for waterfowl was thus saved and as an unplanned bonus, an Ivory-billed woodpecker. But our Government's Army Corps of Engineers never gives up. They are now working on plans to channelize the nearby Arkansas River. Aldo Leopold's message on a land use ethic still has a long way to go before it seeps into official federal policy.

Within the past year or so three books on the ivory-bill have appeared, "The Race to Save the Lord God Bird" by Phillip Hoose, "In Search of the Ivory-billed Woodpecker" by Jerome Jackson" and "The Grail Bird" by Tom Gallagher. first two came out before the re-discovery. Gallagher describes the discovery in great detail since he was among those who claim to have seen it. Recently, Jackson was one of three biologists who questions the evidence so far presented towards confirming the bird's existence. It is normal among scientists to question evidence they consider inadequate. But those who claim to have seen the bird or who accept the poor photographic and sound records will fight back, so the debate is on. There is much at stake on who wins the debate because huge amounts of publicity, money, time and reputation are involved.

Jim Tanner's intensive study of the Ivory-bill in the late

1930's provides the best information in print about the Ivory-bill. In 1944 an artist, Don Eckelberry made sketches of the Ivory-bill at the last known stronghold of this rare bird before the Singer Tract was stripped of its virgin timber. This according to Tim Gallagher in his book "The Grail Bird" was the last accepted sighting of the Ivory-bill on American soil- until 2004. Yes, there were other reports of sightings in between these dates, some particularly one by John Dennis in the Big Thicket of Texas were likely valid but not convincingly documented. So the recent record of a sighting shook the world of bird-watchers as no previous event ever has.

What would you do if you stumbled on the first sighting of a bird long considered extinct? The first responders to this news played their part well. Somehow they kept it a secret for nearly a year. But the dilemma was unbearable. In his excellent book about the hunt for and finding of this bird, Gallagher describes the feeling by those closest to it, after the discovery:

"As the new field season begins (2005) and researchers fan out across Bayou de View and White River, I'm full of excitement and eager to get back to Arkansas. But I also feel heartsick in some ways. I often think of Marty Scott's words: "I hope you have the smartness to do the right thing... If you make the sightings know you doom the bird. So far, we've shown as a species that we're incapable of doing the right thing...I want to think that you will do the right thing this time."

What is the right thing? In the last chapter of his book he wrote: "As I begin the final chapter of this narrative (about the rediscovery) it is the last day of November 2004 and three fifteen-passenger vans chuck full of field equipment have shoved off from Cornell's Lab of Ornithology loading bay en route to Arkansas."

What was the federal response? The spring 2005 issue of Fish & Wildlife News, a USFWS publication tells us. "April 28, 2005, was a historic day for wildlife conservation with the announcement of a confirmed existence of an Ivory-billed woodpecker in Arkansas... the challenge for the Service at the moment will be to manage the influx of birders from all over the world who will want to see the bird. The best opportunity for birders to add this bird to their life list is in the adjacent Dagmar Wildlife Management Area... Good viewing areas are designated in the associated map. The Service is working with the Arkansas Game and Fish Commission; Arkansas Natural Heritage Commission and the Nature Conservancy to provide additional viewing sites, which are expected to be available in early May... Responding to the dramatic rediscovery of the Ivory-billed woodpecker, Secretary Gale Norton and Agriculture Secretary Mike Johanns announced a multi-year, multi-million dollar partnership effort to aid the rare bird's survival. (These two departments) have proposed that more than 10 million in Federal funds be committed to protect the bird (to) supplement 10 million already committed to research and habitat protection efforts by private sector groups and citizens, an amount expected to grow as news of the rediscovery spreads ... The future of the Ivory-billed woodpecker is far from guaranteed. One thing that is certain however, the FWS will play a critical role if we do succeed in bringing this great bird back from the brink of extinction".

The announcement of the finding of the Ivory-bill unleashed a firestorm of people and money, flowing toward the scene like a tidal wave. Will this benefit or eliminate the ivory-bill? In his book, Gallagher describes the fate awaiting those who claimed to have seen an Ivory-bill but are unable to produce adequate proof. Even highly respected ornithologists who claimed seeing this bird have been ridiculed by their colleagues. Now, three biologists have stepped forward and questioned the evidence.

If their challenge holds up, it would undermine a scientific triumph. However it will unleash a fierce rebuttal from the claimers. A fight such as this could upset the apple cart both for would-be protectors and for the bird, itself.

Since Leopold's time, wildlife management agencies have had considerable experience in bringing back rare species from the brink of extinction. Among the most spectacular examples are the Whooping Crane and the Condor. There have been failures, too, such as with the Thick-billed parrot but the batting average is quite good. Miracles in the bird world can happen and rediscovery of the Ivory-bill is one of them but the prognosis for bringing them back is not good. So far everything is based on the sighting of one bird and now even that is being debated. Recovery programs require lots of money and broad public support. The Ivory-bill program already has both money and support, but what is the next step toward doing the right thing? The first step is to confirm that the species still exists and major efforts to do so are either in progress or planned for the near future. Unless new evidence is found to quiet the critics, there will be growing numbers of skeptics and shrinking support for a recovery program. However much already has been gained in the form of habitat protection for many species other than the Ivory-bill and the world has learned a lesson in the importance of habitat protection.

I find it disappointing that according to the federal response statement quoted above, the Fish and Wildlife Service's first thought was to provide viewing opportunities for the expected influx of birders. No bird in history has ever been more successful in dodging observations by bird watchers and even professionals so the idea of establishing viewing areas for large numbers of people to see this bird seems far-fetched. It is nice to know that both the Department of the Interior and of Agriculture are supportive of the Ivory-bill recovery program, but that the Army Corps of Engineers is working on plans to channelize the nearby Arkansas River indicates a lack of uniformity in Federal policy toward conservation matters, a failure that Leopold pointed out 70 years ago.

On May 11, 1947, a monument was erected at Wyalusing State Park in Wisconsin in memory of the passenger pigeon, a case of doing the right thing but too late. At the dedication, Aldo Leopold delivered one of his most memorable speeches. Here's an extract from that speech:

"For one species to mourn the death of another is a new thing under the sun. The Cro-Magnon who slew the mammoth thought only of steaks. The sportsman who shot the last pigeon thought only of his prowess. The sailor who clubbed the last awk thought of nothing at all. But we, who have lost the pigeons, mourn the loss. Had the funeral been ours, the pigeons would hardly of mourned us. In this fact, rather than in Mr. Vandevar Bush's bombs, or Mr. DuPont's nylons, lies objective evidence of our superiority over the beasts."

Let's hope that the Ivory-bill story has a more cheerful ending.

In the case of this Ivory-bill, maybe the right thing to have done would have been to do nothing. Now that option is lost.

*****

For no better reason than my own curiosity, I analyzed Parts 1 and 2 of *A Sand County Almanac* from the viewpoint of Leopold's commitment to ornithology as reflected by the birds he mentions. Part I tells experiences at the Shack. His foreword sets the stage perfectly. "For us of the minority, the opportunity to see geese is more important than television, and the chance to find a pasque flower is a right as inalienable as free speech:"

Part I then goes through the 12 months of the year with my extract from an essay about each as follows:

January (*January Thaw*)
"One may follow a skunk track or search for bands on the chickadees or see what young pines the deer have browsed, or what muskrat houses the mink have dug..."

February (*Good Oak*)
"Now our saw bites into the 1800s... We cut 1899 when the last passenger pigeon collided with a charge of shot near Babcock... Rest! Cries the chief sawyer, and we pause for breath."

March (*The Geese Return*)
"One swallow does not make a summer, but one skein of geese cleaving the murk of a March thaw, is the spring".

April (*Come High Water*)
"I know of no solitude so secure as one guarded by a spring flood; nor do the geese, who have seen more kinds and degrees of aloneness than I have".

May (*Sky Dance*)

"The curtain goes up one minute later each day until 1 June... This sliding scale is dictated by vanity, the dance demanding a romantic light intensity of exactly 0.05 foot candles. Do not be late, and sit quietly, lest he fly away in a huff".

June (*The Alder Fork*)

"In the fresh of the morning, when a hundred white throats had forgotten that it would ever again be anything but sweet and cool, I climbed down the dewy bank and stepped into the Alder Fork".

July (*Great Possessions*)

"We sally forth, the dog and I, at random... Now he is going to translate for me the olfactory poems... At the end of each poem sits the author if we can find him. What we actually find is...a woodcock..."

August (*The Green Pasture*)

"As this dries slowly in the sun, goldfinches bathe in its pools, and deer, herons, killdeers, raccoons and turtles cover it with a lacework of tracks".

September (*The Choral Copse*)

"By September, the day breaks with little help from birds. A song sparrow may give a single half-hearted song, a woodcock my twitter overhead...a barred owl may terminate the night's argument with one last wavering call, but few other birds have anything to say or sing about".

October (*Smoky Gold*)
"There are two kinds of hunting: ordinary hunting and ruffed-grouse hunting. There are two places to hunt grouse: ordinary places and Adams County".

November (*A Mighty Fortress*)
"My woods houses a dozen ruffed-grouse but during periods of deep snow my grouse shift to my neighbor's woods where there is better cover... A flock of a dozen chickadees spends the year in my woods. In winter, when we are harvesting diseased or dead trees, the ring of the axe is dinner gong for the chickadee tribe".

December (*65290*)
"The chickadees that visit our feeding station are trapped and banded each winter...65290 was one of 7 chickadees constituting the class of 1937" "65290 has long since gone to his reward. I hope that in his new woods, great oaks full of ants' eggs keep falling all day long, with never a wind to ruffle his composure or take the edge off his appetite and I hope that he still wears my band".

So ends Part I. Birds are mentioned in 60 of the 92 pages.

Part II: Sketches Here and There are essays of Leopold experiences from Mexico to Canada. Of the 15 essays in this part, five are mostly about birds. Birds are mentioned on 42 of its 67 pages so in Parts I and II together nearly 2 pages out of 3 contain reference to one or more birds and 80 bird species are mentioned. Perhaps ASCA qualifies as a bird book since it is so rich in bird lore!

But the Professor's expertise as an ornithologist doesn't end there. He used birds or their songs liberally as historical and phenology benchmarks.

In his paper "Wisconsin Wildlife Chronology" published in 1940, Leopold consulted 43 sources on the history of wildlife to illustrate how the advance of civilization in Wisconsin had impacted wildlife from 1822-1940. He cites 198 events to document this process and, of these, 78 involved birds. Leopold was a master at using wildlife, particularly birds, in using history to help explain and often solve present-day dilemmas.

The science of phenology also fascinated him, as evidenced by his paper with S.E. (Sara) Jones published in 1947- "A phenological record for Sauk and Dane counties, Wisconsin 1935-45". His daughter, Nina, has continued this record and with it demonstrated the effects of global warming. But it was his final major study in bird song that caused him great satisfaction but much loss of sleep. His paper co-authored with Alfred E. Eynon, entitled "Avian daybreak and evening song in relation to time and light intensity" was published posthumously in 1961. The authors recorded the singing of 20 species of songbirds involving a total of 804 early mornings and 164 evenings. Leopold recorded the day break songs on 345 days mainly between 1944 and 1947. Think what this means in terms of dedication and sleep-loss! The co-author stated that "Leopold was often up and about more than an hour and a half before sunrise". Think also of his many commitments and accomplishments during regular daylight hours and during many evenings!

My work over the years has put me in touch with numerous ornithologists but Aldo Leopold was unique. He was not an artist but he could word-paint birds and find more uses for birds than anyone else I ever knew. Game birds were his bread and butter, just as they have been for me, but certain non-game birds have fascinated him as his essays clearly show. Certainly, he wore his ornithologist hat with great distinction.

15

A SAD TELEGRAPH & LETTER (1948)

As mentioned earlier, Art kept meticulous files including correspondence from the Professor, his colleagues, and friends. I ran across the following two pieces of correspondence, a telegraph from Oak Park, IL and a letter written four days later from the University of Wisconsin - Madison. On April 21, 1948 Aldo Leopold had died while fighting a grass fire on a neighbor's farm near the shack. Art was working at the Delta Waterfowl Research Station in Manitoba. On April 23, 1948 Art received the following telegraph:

OAK PARK, ILL 905 A APRIL 23 1948
ARTHUR HAWKINS,
DELTA WATERFOWL RESEARCH STATION,
DELTA, MAN.

YOU GUYS KEEP YOUR CHINS UP. WE ARE ON OUR OWN NOW. GRAB THAT TORCH. DIG DEEPER. PHENOLOGY FOREVER.
BOB MANN

A few days later, a letter dated April 27th, addressed to Mr. H. Albert Hochbaum, et al. was sent to the Delta research station in Manitoba, where Art and other friends of the Professor were stationed. Signed by Robert A. McCabe, Instructor in Professor Leopold's department at the University of Wisconsin, it read as follows:

Dear Albert,

Now that the immediate shock of Professor Leopold's death has passed, Pat Murrish, Barbara Rogers (the Professor's secretaries) and I thought some of his close friends would you like to know some of the details of the tragedy. This is not meant to be a morbid recital of facts, but we feel that by knowing some of these facts the tensions that accompany an event like this will be somewhat lessened.

In brief, the story is as follows.

Prior to the spring vacation which started April 17, Aldo had been run down considerably by a series of events, the most important of which were overwork and unaccountable reoccurrences of facial disorder. He left Friday afternoon for the shack with the intention of spending at least ten days in relaxation and in planting a small pine plantation. Mrs. Leopold and Estella accompanied him. He apparently was enjoying the stay at the shack and had begun to plant some of the pines. On the morning of April 21 a rather large grass fire got started on a neighbor's property. This was about eight o'clock. At about ten o'clock the fire began to threaten a neighbor's mink ranch. Aldo, with other neighbors, began to gather to help combat the blaze. Mrs. Leopold warned Aldo not to participate. To this Aldo replied that in a case such as this, there was nothing to do but to go and help. It was almost like a conditioned reflex with him. He apparently took an active part in the fighting, although he was at the time, somewhat apart from the major burning. It is alleged that the wind shifted, and strengthen the fire at the point where he had been working.

When he did not report at the shack for lunch, Mrs. Leopold and Estella became concerned, and went to a neighbor to inquire about Aldo's whereabouts. A small remaining group of men began to search for him and the man who actually found the body showed exceptional foresight in that he did not call attention to it, but instead took Mrs. Leopold back to the shack. He then returned and took the body to the farmhouse. The Sauk County Coroner ruled beyond all doubt, Aldo died of a heart attack. This was undoubtedly brought on by his weakened condition, exertion, and heat. The unfortunate thing was that after Aldo collapsed the fire passed his body, and he was therefore badly burned.

Needless to say, his close friends rallied in a hurry so that Mrs. Leopold was well taken care of in those first hectic twenty-four hours after the accident. Young Estella held up like a trooper, and was a great comfort to her mother. His sons Carl and Starker were able to come home from Massachusetts and California respectively. The third son, Luna, whose wife is expecting a baby, was unable to get here from Hawaii. Likewise, his daughter Nina, who is also expecting a baby momentarily, was unable to leave Columbia, Missouri.

To eliminate the mental strain of double funeral services, none was held in Madison. No flowers were also requested. The body was taken to Burlington, Iowa on Friday, April 23, and was buried in Aspen Grove Cemetery in the Starker plot (Aldo's mother's maiden name). The cemetery is an old one, and the Starker Platt is on a little Knoll, and Aldo's grave is below two tall white pines.

From Madison, Professor Roark, Joe Hickey and I acted as pallbearers. The day was a beautiful one. The services were short, simple, and impressive.

These are the facts.

We are now attempting to carry on as best we can where Aldo left off. It is obvious that we are rattling around in his shoes. There is, however, one idea that seems to be in the minds of most of us, and that is that somewhere, somehow, we would like to have a memorial for the Professor. At this point, I would like only to implant the idea and hope that if ideas occur to any of his friends, we should be very glad to hear about them.

Sincerely yours,

Bob

Robert A. McCabe

Instructor

A handwritten note followed:

Dear Al:

This letter is one of a number sent to his close friends. It is only meant to give details that you folks at Delta would like to know. Our hearts here are still heavy.

Bob

16

ART'S LAST LETTER (2006)

Art Hawkins passed away on March 9th, 2006 at the age of 92. His life ended in a most fitting way - after a glorious spring outing, hiking with his dog Koko and sitting on his marsh bench visiting with dear granddaughter Piper. Later in the day, daughter Amy found him lying on the ground near their barn, walking sticks in hand and binoculars around his neck. Art died while doing exactly what he loved to do and lived for each day of his life.

Art's last letter arrived in my mailbox on March 10th. The day after I learned of his passing on March 9th from daughter Amy. The letter was dated March 7th. Needless to say, I was trembling when I opened the envelope and read his final words to me.

Dear Ken:

The busy weekend is over. Ours went well. How about yours? The Pembletons were here the night before they left for Wisconsin. They planned to visit 4 of the "Read Leopolds" and regretted not being able to fit in yours. I shared your letter with them including the excellent pics of Erik and his brant and kissing goodbye to the timberdoodle. Erik is off to a flying start with the background you've given him. Have you had any official reaction to a dog display (Gus) at the new (ALF) building? I agree that dogs played an important part in Leopold's activities in general (back to his boyhood days) so always was important to Aldo. I can see it now – a lifesize pic of Aldo and Gus surveying Great Possessions at daybreak. Or, Gus on point at the corner overlooking Crawfish Prairie.

We're out of horses. Amy's 28 yr old "Peach" died suddenly on 2/15, the coldest night of the year. When Amy came home from school (where she serves as a "para") that afternoon Peach was down. The vet couldn't help so they put her down. A sad day.

You probably know Mark Martin who works for the DNR on prairie restoration and lives at and manages the Goose Pond Sanctuary for Madison Audubon. He was here for our annual wood duck society meeting and spent considerable time with Betty and me briefing us on all the restoration work being done by Madison Audubon around Faville Grove and Lake Mills, in partnership with several agencies including Pheasants Forever. Ed had given me one of the new Leopold posters which we exhibited at our meeting and told the group about the Read Leopolds going on in Wisconsin that day. We had about 80 people there, several from Wisconsin. Our main speaker was Dave Zentner whom you may have heard at Stevens Point a year ago. His was a great presentation on the importance of wetlands and failures of legislators to do their part. I suggested a Read Leopold day in MN. With legislators invited to do the reading. They need it!

Amy is heading a committee putting on a LEP workshop at Wolf Ridge next month and is working with the banquet committee of the Lady Slipper chapter of Pheasants Forever.

Also Ed told her that they received some money to put on a workshop for teachers at the White Bear Lake school district sometime this spring – another job for Amy who keeps plenty busy as para working with kids that have learning disabilities or just plain rebels against the system and refuse to try. Some kids are downright dangerous. Most of the problems are with the parents.

Your "sky dance" theme for a workshop sounds like a winner. Woodcock are due back any day now at least around springs. Our landscape is white from a recent half-incher but bare spots will appear late today if the temp reaches 35 or so. Our local turkey flock still numbers 5, last time I saw it last Friday and a few geese are back but no robins or blackbirds yet. At sunset yesterday Amy counted 30 crows fly overhead north.

Ellen's place up north has been interesting. They dragged in a couple of road-killed deer where they could see them from their house. Two fishers found them first. Later another fisher, 2 foxes, marten and then 2 wolves took over with a bunch of ravens. They saw the fishers take to nearby trees when the wolves moved in. Last time they were here, they brought us a freshly shed moose antler, a dandy. Rich picked it up on his way to work one morning. Later Ellen went back with snowshoes to track the moose on the off-chance she'd find the other antler. She did find it about 100 yards in from the road. What luck! Not much new on the Ivory-bill.

Best wishes,
Art

Before Art left this world on that glorious spring day, one can only dream he saw his first spring robin, blackbird and was witness to a woodcock performing a "sky dance".

If not, rest assured, Art Hawkins and Betty are busy and in charge of monitoring all things wild and wonderful inhabiting their neck of the hereafter.

17

EPILOGUE

Not only was Art Hawkins a biologist, ornithologist, writer and journalist, he was a bit of a poet and theologist in his own right. On January 17, 2000, he recalled Leopold words in a poem he penned to commemorate the raising of a new family barn in Hugo.

The Book and The Shack*
Art Hawkins

This is the year we celebrate
the Book renowned worldwide as great.
At first this Book got little mention
But now it draws worldwide attention.

The present year is ninety nine
Toast it with the finest wine!

The symbol of the Book, the Shack,
Possesses features others lack.

Simple both in size and form,
It keeps its builders dry and warm
Midst summer's rain and winter's storm.

Great Possessions, this Shack exuded
A wealth of memories included
The Book and Shack are tied together
As closely bound as by a tether
From chicken coop to worldly shrine
The Shack still stands amidst the pine.

So as not to cause confusion
The painting's Amy's contribution
With salvaged boards from our old barn
(Some rotten ones aren't worth a darn)
Tom framed the painting of the Shack
If you don't like it we'll take it back.

I will admit I wrote this verse
If you agree it could be worse.

* It was on January 12, 1935, the day after Aldo's forty-eighth birthday, that Aldo and his friend Ed Ochsner "discovered" the chicken coop that became the world-famous Shack, the Mecca for all true conservationists.

Ten days earlier I first met Aldo and his family, and became his third student. Leonard Wing and Franklin Schmidt were already there, and Vivian Horn was Aldo's Secretary, in the new Department of Game Management.

The raising of our new barn this month will become a monument to the starting point in *A Sand County Almanac*.

Amy Dolin's painting of the Shack will serve as another reminder of what can evolve from a simple start. I hope that this will be the year that the Foundation and Leopold Education Project come to a happy arrangement.

*****

Art and Betty lived in an old farmhouse on the banks of Lake Amelia near Hugo, Minnesota. Fondly referred to as "The Farm" by family members, it embodied their lifestyle and devotion to the environment they so loved. Another book could be written describing Art and his family's fight to preserve and protect the land surrounding the lake from developers. Except for the sound of nearby automobile traffic, one would be hard pressed to imagine they were not at a northwoods retreat. The kitchen window overlooked the lake, the yard was surrounded by well-used wood duck nesting boxes and the deck harbored many worn bird feeders - never empty of feathered visitors - including several pileated woodpeckers and fur covered raccoons.

After Art passed away in 2006, Amy Hawkins Dolin and her mother Betty, as I mentioned earlier, graciously allowed me access to her father's office and files at their home on the lake. Besides interviewing Art and Betty several times at their farmhouse on the lake, I also had chance to ask Amy several questions to fill in the blanks. One evening we discussed her father's religious leanings.

"He was raised a Methodist," she said. "And while we children grew up, the family attended a Presbyterian church in

White Bear Lake." She noted that her father formed a committee on Environmental Programs in Churches (EPIC) there in 1970. There they had a semi trailer in the parking lot for collection of paper, plastic and glass in barrels for recycling.

During the last five years of his life Amy often caught him reading the Bible and noticed her father become much more philosophical. "He enjoyed the provocative questions and how they wrote."

Amy, as Art mentioned often in his letters to me, has devoted her professional career to environmental education. She, along with her siblings Tex and Ellen, share their father's and mother's love for nature. Tex, retired now after a long, distinguished career with the US Fish & Wildlife Service - Ellen, living the good life in the woods near Ely, Minnesota, where she's a retired wilderness ranger with the U.S. Forest Service out of Tofte. Can you hear Art's voice in Amy's recent essay?

Late summer on the farm. Foofie and Fitzi love quiet Saturday mornings like this. I can hear black walnuts dropping in the woods as squirrels busily cut them; "crash, shudder, THUD" and shots firing (it's early goose season) from hunting parties tucked away in remnant hay fields around the neighborhood.

The big bluestem is stunning now- consistent summer rains made it lush, ocre/burgundy and so graceful in the breeze; the prairie is alive with crickets, sparrows and butterflies. Migration is in full swing with lots of warblers flitting around in the woods' edge and hawks riding thermals against intense blue skies. It's fun to lie in the hammock on the hill and watch them dreamily drift by... and it's not just the hawks, pelicans and eagles but also Monarchs on their way to Mexico and spiders riding silver webs— where are they going?!... another of nature's great mysteries!

EPILOGUE

Our pair of Sandhill Cranes spent the entire summer here, loafing and poking around after worms and frogs and lying in the shade. They were so calm and fun. Their nest failed in June so both birds spent their time on the lawn and in the silo pond mostly. They'd hop and dance and bugle feet from the deck, treating us to the best show on earth. They're gone now; have been for about a week- maybe wintering in Bosque Del Apache Refuge in New Mexico.

The osprey tower is quiet now, too; I think our female has left for her Central or South American wintering grounds. Mom leaves first, and then dad and the (3) kids follow. They don't migrate together as far as we know. She may winter in Panama while he may winter in Costa Rica... the kids are on their own. We know this from radio transmitter research.

The loons also appear to be gone-they had one big, fat, gray loonlet. And the Trumpeter swans with their five signets are still here and doing well. We worry about them when hunters venture onto the marsh in late September — does everyone know the difference between silhouette geese and swans before sunrise when they shoot? Not always. We hope they all survive hunting season as the huge, awkward babies learn to fly so late in the season (terrified and confused amidst the barrage of shooters).

I can hear lots of chickadees, blue jays, robins, a cat bird, goldfinches and red squirrels... bright golden leaves are cartwheeling down from the walnuts on this warm, dry breeze as this perfect weekend begins!

I hope you're all doing well and enjoying the day.
Always, from the farm, Amy

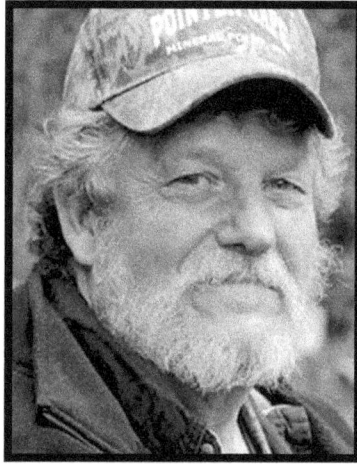

Ken M. Blomberg is a freelance writer and longtime resident of Junction City in north central Wisconsin. Author of three books, *Up the Creek*, *Wisconsin Bird Hunting Tales*, and now *Letters from Art*, his freelance articles have been published in *Field & Stream*, *Pointing Dog Journal*, *Fur, Fish & Game*, *Wing & Shot* and the *Ruffed Grouse Society (RGS)* magazine – as well as state publications like *Wisconsin Sportsman*, *Badger Sportsman*, and *Woods and Waters*. He is a 1976 graduate of UWSP in Resource Management and past Executive Director of the Wisconsin Rural Water Association. Ken, now retired, writes a weekly outdoor column for the *Portage County Gazette* and owns a gun dog kennel in the heart of ruffled grouse and woodcock country.

www.ingramcontent.com/pod-product-compliance
Lightning Source LLC
Chambersburg PA
CBHW032353280326
41935CB00008B/558